IS THAT ME ?

My life with schizophrenia

Anthony Scott

Edited by Susan Dolamore

A. & A. Farmar

British Library Cataloguing in Publication Data
A CIP catalogue record for this book is available from the British Library.

Text designed and set by A. & A. Farmar
Photograph on the title page and back cover by Dean Tobias. All other photographs are reproduced by kind permission of the Scott family.
Cover design by Alice Campbell
Printed and bound by GraphyCems

ISBN 1-899047-91-3

First published in 2002
by
A. & A. Farmar
Beech House
78 Ranelagh Village
Dublin 6
Ireland
Tel: 353 1 496 3625
Fax: 353 1 497 0107
Email: afarmar@iol.ie

Web: farmarbooks.com

Contents

schizophrenia n. a mental disease marked by disconnection between thought, feelings and actions, often with delusions and withdrawal from social relationships. *Oxford English Dictionary*

Foreword

Anthony W. Clare

Over the centuries certain diseases have served to cause particular fear, even terror and have attracted opprobrium, hostility and prejudice. One thinks of the plague, smallpox, syphilis, tuberculosis, leprosy and, in our own time, cancer and Aids. Sufferers from such conditions have not just had to cope with the distressing, debilitating and often fatal symptoms of their disease but have had to endure discrimination and worse arising out of public ignorance and misunderstanding. One condition, which is both serious in its presentation, course and outcome and also stigmatised and neglected by the public, is schizophrenia.

Most disorders which affect our thinking, feelings, perceptions, memories and behaviours frighten us. We talk of 'losing our mind'. Those who experience such disturbances, as well as their families and friends, often feel isolated, vulnerable and misunderstood. These illnesses tend to remain hidden. Those who suffer them are rarely in a position to describe how they are when ill and are even less likely to draw attention to themselves by talking about their experiences when well. The situation is, fortunately, beginning to change. People who have experienced quite serious mental diseases such as bipolar manic depression, anorexia nervosa, alcohol and drug dependence, obsessive compulsive disorder, panic disorder, phobic states, even suicidal tendencies have come forward and written and spoken about their ordeal, treatment and eventual recovery. But there is a great lack of a clear, lucid, authentic and personal account of what it is like to suffer from what is arguably the most severe psychotic illness, namely schizophrenia. Recently, of course, there has been Sylvia Nash's widely praised account of the American mathematical genius, Nobel prizewinner and schizophrenia sufferer, John Nash, but her book, *A Beautiful Mind*, tells the story from the outside looking in. What is sorely needed is an account of what it is like to be inside looking out.

It is this personal perspective as well as its powerful narrative dynamic and painfully honest style that makes Anthony Scott's account of how he developed schizophrenia, how he coped with its slowly developing, sinister and ultimately disastrous effects and how he learned to live a life of astonishing richness and sensitivity, such a jewel. Those who know next to nothing about what it is like to experience terrifying hallucinations as well as those who believe they do, and I include here psychiatrists, nurses and community health workers, will never read a more revelatory and illuminating insight than that provided by Scott. Painstakingly he shows how insidiously his mental state began to deteriorate and how every element of his life, his ambition to be a lawyer, his desire for a personal and intimate relationship, his contact and involvement with his family, was profoundly affected. But it is his searingly honest account of what he terms the 'intolerable agony' that will surprise many who do not automatically associate physical and mental pain with mental illness. Honest too is his frank account of the episodes of violent behaviour that occurred when he was at his most disturbed and fragmented.

A striking feature of Anthony Scott's testimony is his total lack of self-pity. He recognises not alone the toll the illness took of his drive, his ability to relate to others and his willingness to take the advice of others but also the impact of his illness on those around him, his family, friends and on the woman he loved and fellow-patient, Nancy. It was her love for and belief in him that was to make such a crucial contribution to maintaining his fragile hold on life and sanity and from this relationship was born his beloved son, Seán. Some, unfamiliar with schizophrenia and stuck with the completely erroneous view of it as some kind of Jekyll and Hyde, split-personality state, will be surprised at the courage and integrity of this man in the throes of a bewildering fragmentation of his mental processes. There is his touching self-deprecation as when he writes in his diary at one particularly dark point, 'There I go again, screaming like a pig in the darkness of my sty'. There is his astonishing insight as when he remarks how some of his seemingly feckless and irresponsible behaviour must have given people the impression of him as 'being like a backward overgrown schoolboy for whom every day was a holiday'.

Anthony Scott knew at first hand what a psychosis is like. There is in his account no trace of romantic idealisation of the illness as a journey into sanctity nor any apocalyptic endorsement of it as some kind of descent into murderous violence. He had no existential vision, nor did he commit any crime. His account does much to dispel some of the most tenacious and obfuscating misunderstandings concerning the illness. Agony and ecstasy do occur and mingle but much of his experience is of a 'world in limbo' that sufferers of schizophrenia inhabit. In this world, staggering between the more florid exacerbations and crises of his condition, Anthony Scott negotiates a painfully slow and episodic journey to a state of some mental peace and equilibrium

Is that me?

reached in the final years of his life.

What makes this story almost unbearable as a highly intro-spective and truthful account of suffering and triumph is the fact that its author was not to see it published. Anthony Scott died of natural causes two years ago. Reassuring to his family, particularly to his son, Seán, of whom he writes so proudly towards the end of his book, and to his sister, Ciarín, who provided for him what no psychiatrist, however gifted and humane, can provide, namely love seasoned with common sense and endless patience, is the fact that the last years did give him some tranquillity. The final chapter reads like a summation of the good and decent things in his life, his parents, his siblings, his friends, his doctors and nurses, his fellow-patients, Nancy and Seán. He ends his great narrative with the hope that he might recognise the man in the shaving mirror as an old friend. Readers of this wonderfully frank, humorous, sad, moving and generous book can only marvel at his courage and self-knowledge and mourn that they were not privileged to know him as an old friend themselves.

My story

I awoke earlier than usual. It seemed like any other fresh spring day. I went into the bathroom and, as I was shaving, my attention was suddenly arrested by signs of decrepit old age on the face in the shaving mirror. Startled, I paused and looked more closely. The face was yellow and wizened, the chin line indistinct. I wondered how old was the ancient before me. Eighty perhaps? I was shocked. How had he got there? Who was he? Was it the old man from next door come to do the gardening? I awakened from my reverie to see the dry parchment-like lips mouth the words, 'Is that me?' I can tell it is high time I set down the events, people and places in my life, before one morning the face in the shaving mirror slowly crumbles into dust in front of my disbelieving eyes.

My first thought was, who on earth would be interested in the story of a paranoid schizophrenic? However, I remembered being told that the reader tends to be more intelligent than the writer, and is generally on the writer's side. I should like to give my readers an insight into the troubled life I have led and show that it is possible to come to terms even with a disability such as mine.

In 1959, a French friend of mine called schizophrenia '*la maladie de notre siècle*', or the illness which characterises our century, and I believe that he was right. Psychiatrists say that the majority of schizophrenics are no threat to anyone but themselves; indeed it is known that schizophrenia is such a devastating disease that ten per cent of its victims take their own lives rather than face the prospect of indefinite excruciating inward pain and the inability to cope outside an institution. I can understand why the World Health Organization describes the illness as the most painful a human being can go through.

Recent medical opinion has stated that schizophrenia is caused by a chemical imbalance, triggered off psychosomatically in certain young adults, mostly young men, who tend to be fairly bright and also exceptionally sensitive. The Romans called it *dementia praecox*, or madness of the young. It seems to me to be a pretty random chance as to who contracts it. Fortunately, relatively few do. In my own case, as far as I was aware at the time, my first twenty years gave me no indication of what was to come, apart from a vague sense of disaster ahead, inescapable but at this stage devoid of any of the pain unique to schizophrenia.

I inherit my father's lust for life, his ability to get on well with people and, to an extent, his aesthetic sense, but it is from my mother that I inherit my memory, my sense of fair play, and, again to an extent, my intellect, together with my capacity for deep emotion and my sensitivity. Sadly, the last two characteristics have helped to make me prone to schizophrenia.

From the patient's point of view there are, broadly speaking, two main features of this disturbing disease. Firstly, there is the continuous and severe mental pain, which inhibits all contact with the outside world. The other equally relevant feature is that it is difficult, if not impossible, to concentrate for any length of time. Even to begin to do anything helpful at home is too painful to seem worth the effort. All one feels like doing is to sit all day listening to the radio or watching television. Losing oneself in the programme has the effect of calming the brain's hyperactivity and allowing the nightmarish fantasies to recede and fortunately, a minimum of thought is required for this form of escapism. Because of this inability to concentrate, it is usually impossible to hold down a job for more than a short period.

The schizophrenic needs medication that stabilises him and gives him the opportunity to be his old self once again; releasing him to a consciousness of his own personal thoughts and emotional responses concerning the world around him, as coloured by his nature, personality and social conditioning.

We can only be in a position to know and understand others according to how we know and understand ourselves. In my teens, before I was ill, I found that through knowing myself I could also know others and feel a rapport with them. When one has schizophrenia this is impossible.

Though far from being a panacea, today's medication can help and indeed, in my own case, is vital for my quality of life. Equally necessary is informed and structured support in the community, which is still all too often conspicuous by its absence. I myself have been lucky in that for twenty-seven years there was a Good Samaritan in my life. Her moral qualities were rare by any standards. Though our life together was sometimes turbulent, she, more than anyone, gave me the chance of living to old age. This was Nancy. Of Nancy herself and her part in keeping me going on an even keel for so long, there will be more later.

I hope that my story will go some way towards alerting the reader to an understanding of the intolerable agony experienced by the schizophrenic and help to bridge the gap between such sufferers and other people.

1. Geragh

Where to begin? Lewis Carroll has the King of Hearts giving this piece of advice to the White Rabbit: "'Begin at the beginning,' the King said, gravely, 'and go on till you come to the end: then stop.'" I will follow the King's advice.

I was born in London on 10 November 1933 and my mother took me as an infant to my father's and her native Ireland. Her own mother was Irish and her father English; both my father's parents were Irish. I lived in Ireland with my parents and eventually my brothers Michael, Brian and Niall and much younger sister Ciarín until I was nearly twenty-five. Our family home, Geragh, was built in 1938 on a granite quarry by my architect father Michael at Sandycove Point near Dún Laoghaire on Dublin Bay. The family of (then) three children and our parents moved into Geragh as soon as it was ready. The house, named by my father after the valley in County Kerry where our ancestors had lived, is widely regarded as one of the finest examples of the Modern movement in 1930s' architecture. Geragh is a large white house built like the prow of a ship, with balconies, portholes and large picture windows. I remember that the impression one got of Geragh from a distance during the day was of an ocean-going liner in dry dock.

After the war my father bought the Martello Tower overlooking Geragh and the Forty Foot bathing-place, where Joyce had stayed and where he set the first chapter of *Ulysses*. Today the Tower houses the James Joyce Museum established by my father.

My parents were social lions. Their New Year's Eve parties at Geragh were highly sought after. Many well-known personalities in the theatre, the arts and politics who came to Dublin met and were entertained by them. The spacious drawing-room, scene of these celebrated parties, contained a brick fireplace with iron fire-dogs designed by the sculptor Oisín Kelly, a grand piano and comfortable sofas and armchairs covered in white bawneen upholstery. My father designed the drawing-room as the focal point of the house. As he never entered a kitchen anywhere, the design of the kitchen at Geragh, though adequate, was at the bottom of his list of priorities. The garden was large enough for us children to play freely in with our friends. My parents' gardeners seemed to get successively older; the last gardener, shortly before my father died, was ninety-eight. Sandycove Harbour was just outside the main gate and there we played on the sand and swam. Later on we four boys graduated to the Forty Foot round the point. There was a notice at the entrance saying 'No dogs, bicycles or women allowed'. Bathers swam in the Forty Foot all year round in Joyce's 'scrotumtightening sea'. At Christmas there was always a handsome tree in the curve of the drawing-room windows. At night, when the lights of the tree were switched on, it could be seen for a mile along the coast road across Scotsman's Bay and it acted as a beacon to drivers going home late after seasonal festivities in the city eight miles away.

My father had left a promising career as an actor with the Abbey Theatre to become an architect. His design for the Irish Pavilion at the World Fair in New York in 1939 was acknowledged to be outstanding and the Mayor, Fiorello La Guardia, made him an Honorary Freeman of that city. He and his practice designed, among other buildings, the Bank of Ireland, the new Abbey Theatre, Radio Telefís

Éireann, the Cork Opera House, the extension to Galway University and what is widely regarded as his best building, Busáras, the bus terminal in Dublin, near the 18th-century Custom House and the River Liffey docks. When Pope John Paul II said Mass in Dublin's Phoenix Park before a million and a half people, my father's practice designed the High Altar. He was awarded the Royal Institute of British Architects Gold Medal in 1975. The RIBA Committee chose 1975 as that year had been designated as Architectural Heritage Year. Her Majesty the Queen presented the award in person: the only occasion that a reigning monarch has ever done so. This is an award seldom given to people not born in Britain and my father is, to date, the only Irish recipient.

My mother's name was Patricia, or Patty. Her father, Joseph Nixon, was a wealthy businessman from Willoughby-in-the-Wold in Nottinghamshire. Her mother, Ellen, was a Moylett from County Mayo and she herself was born there in Ballyhaunis. She was raven-haired and in her youth was considered to be a great beauty. At one point *The Irish Times* carried a sketch of her to advertise Ponds Face Cream. She was probably the most intelligent woman I have known. She was generally considered to be very well read and had been a brilliant student at Trinity College Dublin in her youth.

During the War my two devout paternal maiden aunts, May and Hilda, used to take my brother Michael and myself on the hour-long tram journey from Geragh in Sandycove to Dublin to hear classical concerts. I remember an incident from this time which would suggest that even at that age, like Nancy later on, I felt strong feelings of compassion for what she would call 'the underdog'. The four of us and a lady friend of my aunts were, as usual, on the top deck of the tram so that Michael and I could see better. As we passed over O'Connell Bridge on the return journey I saw an old tramp sitting with his back to the balustrade begging. People were hurrying by taking no notice of him. I do not know if it was the effect of the great music I had just heard or that I was simply tired, but an enormous wave of sympathy and sadness for the old man came over me and I wept bitterly and inconsolably for the rest of the journey home. Years later May and Hilda told my son that I asked them at the time why the old tramp was suffering and that I had asked them the same question about myself when I first became schizophrenic.

My mother was devoted to her five children and gave each of us a good education. After nannies we had governesses and then my three brothers and I went to a Dublin boys' preparatory school—St Conleth's. My abiding memories of the Headmaster, Bernard Shepherd, are of being sent to his study to be punished for a misdemeanour. As I stood before the portly figure with my hand outstretched, palm upwards, and he raised his arm shoulder high, I used to observe his mortarboard set at a slightly rakish angle and the academic gown on to which fell ash from the cigarette permanently at the side of his mouth. Sometimes, like others before and after me, I managed to withdraw my hand at the last moment. The strap then landed at speed on his ample thigh. This ploy merely prolonged the agony as the next time he held one by the fingertips.

During my schooldays I broke bones and sustained other injuries playing rugby, but my most serious injury happened during the Hilary term of my last year at St Conleth's when I got kicked on the head during a maul. This led to an internal release of fluid which put pressure on my brain and caused headaches. A surgeon friend of my parents, Adam McConnell, operated first on one side of my head to release the fluid and then, because the headaches were only partially relieved, on the other side. As I had been violently sick

after the general anaesthetic the first time, I was given a local anaesthetic for the second. Although I was very drowsy, I could feel the
drill boring a hole in the side of my head and the fluid running past
my ear and down my neck. All the psychiatrists I have seen, from
first to last, have discounted the headaches and the operations as
being contributory factors in my later psychosis.

After St Conleth's, Michael and I went on to study at one of
Ireland's leading boarding-schools, the Benedictine Glenstal Priory
(now an Abbey). I was at Glenstal from January 1947, when I was
just thirteen, until the Easter holidays of 1950 when Michael and I
left to go to school in Switzerland for a year. At Glenstal I was
always near the top of the class, but never quite managed to be
overall first. I was fairly good at the Humanities and especially French,
at which I usually came top. At one year's prize-giving, I was given
a book of La Fontaine's *Fables* for coming first in French in my
class.

My first Headmaster was Father Matthew Dillon, known as 'The
Bear' because of his shaven grey head, gruff manner and firm belief
in the educational merits of flogging. I was flogged on two or three
occasions, kneeling over the bed in his study. The pain was severe.
Father Columba, the next Headmaster, did not believe in flogging,
preferring the carrot to the stick. I was one of those in whom he
took a special interest and he encouraged me to read worthwhile
books, as did my mother.

I reached puberty when I was fourteen early in 1948. At once my
capacity for devout religious faith almost vanished. In recent years
it has come back in a minor, but at least, as in my childhood, a
'living' way. The sexual development of the adolescent in the Ireland of the 1940s, and indeed for many years after, was repressed by
the older generation, especially by the clergy, who were most often

responsible for the development of young people. The majority of parents left where we learned about sex to chance as their own parents had done with them—though they must have known we would learn nothing from the clergy. The theories of the Irish clergy of those days in educating young people, which are now widely understood as misguided, were based on the idea that in making us future upright citizens it was vital to repress our emerging sexuality savagely by any means that sprang to mind. (Our inadequate introduction to sex in those days reminds me of how my father learned to swim: apparently my grandfather threw him into the sea from a Liffey pier.) The confusion I experienced upon reaching puberty can be illustrated by the following three incidents in my life and may serve as early indications of the illness I first became aware of in the autumn of 1953, shortly before my twentieth birthday.

The first incident occurred one Easter while we had a French au pair from Le Havre looking after the youngest children. My parents, the au pair, Marie-Thérèse, and we four boys had just finished dinner and were leaving the dining-room. The last two in the room, Marie-Thérèse and my fourteen-year-old self, were about to leave when Marie-Thérèse closed the door, switched off the lights and, to my astonishment, drew me to her and pressed her lips to mine in what I later heard is known as a French kiss. Though by this stage I was pubescent, I felt no instinctively aroused sexual desire and had yet to learn about sexual intercourse from a Glenstal friend, so what might have happened came to nothing. When my school-friend described the sex act to me later on I thought it was something dirty. Today I believe that had Marie-Thérèse, or any other girl, and I had sex around then, in releasing some of my inhibitions this might have lessened the severity of my illness when it finally struck.

Another incident which may have some bearing on my illness

occurred a little later when I was in the Glenstal sick-bay for some minor complaint. During the half hour between games and supper, there was a group of boys outside the sick-bay window discussing the relative sporting abilities of others not present, and I heard Dermot Kelly, a formidable scholar and rugby player from the class above mine, say when it came to my turn to be commented on, 'Oh, Scott? He's a chronic invalid'. This remark, coming from such a source, probably had as punishing an effect on my acutely sensitive nature in the longer term as did my abortive 'affair' with Marie-Thérèse. Indeed, with the arrival of adolescence at that time, I had already begun to sense that I was falling into what appeared to be a very deep pit. Dermot Kelly's words to such an audience sounded another knell for what I vaguely saw as my impending and inevitable doom.

During the summer of 1948 my parents drove my brothers, Michael, Brian and myself in my father's Adler to some of northwest France's seaside resorts. The holiday must have been in July, as I remember reading about the London Olympic Games in the French papers. On our return journey we were staying in Trouville, which borders immediately on to its more fashionable next-door neighbour, Deauville. Before lunch on our first morning, we boys were paddling in the sea while the tide was out. When we returned to our parents on the beach, I found myself, for no apparent reason and for the first and only time, saying something discourteous, ugly and extremely hurtful to my poor mother, whose extreme sensitivity I have inherited. My father's reaction was one of shock and disbelief that I should speak to my mother in a manner so unbecoming and out of character, but he dealt with the situation calmly. To his credit, and fortunately for us, his children, he was not given to violence. Some fathers might have reacted differently on such an occasion, if only in anger and on the spur of the moment.

It is possible that these apparently unrelated events which occurred during my teens were the first signs of the illness which finally overwhelmed me.

Sport was an important part of my life at Glenstal, particularly table-tennis, tennis and rugby. In 1949 there were about a hundred boys altogether at the school and that year, when I was still fifteen, I delighted myself and my friends by overcoming stiff opposition to win the school Table-Tennis Handicap with a handicap of minus seven, and then the Championship.

When my father was at the Jesuits' Belvedere College in Dublin he was the only boy ever to play on both their Junior and Senior Rugby Cup winning teams. My own enjoyment of rugby emphasises the great resemblance I bore to him. Both of us played wing-forward; like my father I was small for my age and like him I was a fearless tackler regardless of the size of the boy bearing down on me. I played in the school under-sixteens team for a couple of seasons. Fortunately, in later years I kept hold of the courage I acquired at Glenstal. It became a moral courage that saw me through the long dark years of ultra-severe schizophrenia.

Over Easter in 1950 Michael and I went to Rome in a school party with Father Columba to celebrate the Holy Year, the *Anno Santo*. In Rome we stayed in a convent and one night after lights-out I slipped out with two other boys and went on a drinking spree. We drank Chianti; I had never drunk alcohol before and became violently sick. I have not drunk Chianti since. As we were returning to the convent a couple of *carabinieri* stopped us. They asked me to show that I could walk along a straight white line in the middle of the road. When I did this they let us go.

I thought that Rome was a beautiful city and especially loved walking along the banks of the Tiber at twilight. We saw the usual tourist attractions and received the Papal blessing from Pope Pius XII from the Vatican balcony in St Peter's Square; I was particularly impressed by the ornate splendour of St Peter's Basilica. My two weeks in Rome were a time I look back on even now with great fondness. I was a young, happy-go-lucky teenager, typical of my generation, enjoying my discovery of the world outside Ireland.

We returned home to find that our parents had had a difference of opinion with the Headmaster which resulted in us being taken away from Glenstal before the start of term. We were sent for our last school year to a Swiss international boys' school, the Institut Montana, on a mountain above Zug in the north-western foothills of the Alps. The sons of comfortably-off parents from all over the world went there, including a fair-haired young tearaway who was Count Ciano's son and Benito Mussolini's grandson. Michael and I were the only Irish boys and I enjoyed the experience of meeting boys from all sorts of different cultures and races. The atmosphere in the school was easy-going, there was no flogging or harsh discipline and I enjoyed my time there very much. I was popular and energetic, playing tennis with some success—to myself, my many friends and my family I was completely normal.

In the Michaelmas Term an Italian boy of about my own age invited me to go with him into the town of Zug, at the foot of our mountain, the Zugerberg, to visit a tea-room where there were call-girls. Whether it was the vestiges of my religious faith or the fact that since I had reached puberty I had received no responsible guidance whatsoever about sex, either at home or at school, I do not know, but I declined. My reaction to Lombroso's invitation was partly fear of the unknown, but I knew it would have been morally wrong to accept and it would have been against the norm of social convention. However, I could not help wondering what unknown delights I might be foregoing.

One of my friends, Paddy Herbst, invited me to his home in Berlin for the Easter holidays in 1951. Most of the bombed and shelled buildings had not yet been rebuilt. Paddy's German father, Walter, and his Irish mother, Julia, made me very welcome. One Sunday the family took me by train through the Eastern Sector to Potsdam in East Germany, to see the beautiful gardens and fine buildings of Frederick the Great's Palace of Sans Souci. When later on I fell ill the Herbst family and my own family remained firm friends.

On my return to the Institut Montana for the Trinity term I had the idea of writing to my parents asking them to send me some Scottish bagpipes, as I wished to impress my school friends. Instead, they, being patriotic, arranged for lessons for me on the Irish or 'uileann' bagpipes when I went home for the summer holidays. At the end of the initial course the tutor pointed out that, while he could see I was keen, mastery of the uileann pipes was beyond me, and the lessons were discontinued. Here was the first indication that music would not be my forte. This is something I have always regretted. Perhaps what Sir Thomas Beecham said of his English audiences applies to me: I don't understand music, but I like the noise it makes. Were I in particularly good form today and tried to sing before a few friends, they might be forgiven for thinking I was suffering from a pain somewhere.

2. The turning point

From 1951 to 1952 I did a *stage*, or course of study, in Christian Philosophy and the History of Fine Art at Louvain University in Belgium. As Louvain is in the Walloon region, the lectures were in French and my knowledge of the language improved considerably. As part of the Philosophy course I studied Ontology, the theory of existence, and Epistemology, the theory of knowledge. Early on in my year's *stage* at Louvain I made friends with two fellow students, Jack, an American veteran of the Korean War, which was then still going on, and Ed, a Canadian. The three of us were studying Christian Philosophy and we had many long conversations, discussing Socrates, Plato's *Dialogues* and Aristotle until dawn. We became firm friends. When I swam in the 400 metres freestyle for Louvain at a Belgian inter-varsity meeting, Jack nearly fell into the pool while urging me on. In the event, I was delighted to finish the course and only come second last, as I had never swum competitively before.

Towards the end of my spring term the three of us decided to do a hitchhiking tour of Europe. We planned our tour throughout the summer term and on the day appointed for our departure I waited for them at my flat, as arranged. When after two or three hours they had not arrived, I set out without further ado on my own. I covered roughly three thousand miles in twenty-one days, on £21. I had to be back in Brussels Airport to catch my return flight to Dublin which had been booked in advance. During my journeys several girls made encouraging advances towards me in a way which a less repressed eighteen-year-old might have found irresistible.

I have no idea why my fellow travellers did not turn up, but I have since wondered whether my impending illness might have been more apparent to these relatively detached students outside Ireland than it was once I was at home again: I was a student in Dublin for two-and-a-half years before people had any idea that there was something radically wrong with me, and then it was as a result of my particularly abnormal behaviour in the summer of 1956. Looking back I see that my move to Louvain was disastrous for my mental health. On my own, in a less protective environment than I had been used to, and studying abstract and challenging subjects at a relatively young age (seventeen at the start of the course), I was isolated and vulnerable.

My year in Belgium was followed by the first year of a degree course in Architecture at University College, Dublin (UCD). At the end of that academic year, I decided that my gifts, such as they were, more resembled the aural talents of my mother than the visual ones of my father. I set my sights, therefore, on a career in politics and at the Bar.

I became ill very slowly from the autumn of 1953; I was twenty in November and had just started to read for an honours degree in Economics at UCD. In the following year I added a concurrent barrister's course at the King's Inns. I wonder today if the impact of my impending illness could have been alleviated had there been anyone close to me to read the danger signs evident on occasion as I grew up, a prey to the repression of a closed Irish Catholic society and my own faltering inhibitions. Maybe with help my illness might have been averted if anyone had been alerted to my condition even after the end of my year at Louvain. My parents had invested all their hopes in me and were proud of my achievements. They will have been unable to allow themselves to realise my predicament. I had always been close to my mother and my illness was impossible for her to accept. My father at this period was very busy and rarely at home. Ireland was then an emerging nation which ten years later would start to attract the attention of the world's leading countries. Even before the War my father had begun to make a name for himself and when, after the War, Ireland became a Republic, he was one of the select group who were to be largely responsible for her successful coming-of-age. Unlike my mother, he judged people, even his own children, less on moral behaviour or lack of it (provided we did not commit a crime) than on our ability to be achievers of note in life. Nor did the prevailing meritocratic climate, at home and at school and university, favour anyone in my family observing the warning signs in a way that a more objectively minded person might have done.

From 1952 to 1956 while I was at UCD I played and enjoyed sport of many kinds. I still played wing-forward in rugby though now only in one of the minor teams. I played a lot of tennis on the Dublin circuit and greatly improved my game from my Glenstal days. For much of the year I threw the javelin on the University playing-fields, then at Belfield, and progressed to the point where I was told that if I continued to improve at such a rate, I would soon be awarded a place on the Athletics Team and a Blue. Sadly, Fate had other plans.

I also took up boxing at university. I strongly suspect that I would not have done so had I not by then begun to feel alienated from my native self, as it was unlike me to express myself in such a way. Perhaps that was why I found waiting for my contest to start more purgatorial than the other boxers did. As far as I remember, I fought seven contests and won three. According to the press, two of my contests were lost on split decisions because 'Scott left his effort too late'.

In alternate years our team boxed against Oxford and Cambridge in England and the following year they fought against us in Dublin. When the team was in Oxford I stayed the night in Keble College. When we were in Cambridge we were entertained at the Hawks' Club, which can only be entered by University Blues. In addition to being awarded a Blue, I was fortunate in winning the Irish Senior Universities' Light-Welterweight Boxing Title one year. I suspect the fact that I got a bye into the Final and thus only had one contest was an advantage.

Really, the only boxing contest from which I emerged with any credit at all was my first. This was against a student from our arch rival university, Trinity College, Dublin. The match was in the UCD Students' Union, Newman House, so our team had the advantage of boxing on home ground. My opponent was a West African called Onojobi. The contest revolved around physical fitness between two inexperienced but determined opponents. The home crowd urged me on as they were never to do again. I won on a split decision. Afterwards I was so overcome by the strain of my efforts that I went into the gardens and was very sick.

Eventually my father told me that unless I was going to be an outstanding boxer, which obviously was not the case, I should give up the sport. Looking back I realise I was lucky not to have been seriously hurt.

From the start of my First Year Economics course in 1953 I sensed a sea-change slowly coming over my personality. I had always tended to be gregarious and was very popular. Now in spite of myself, I found myself becoming withdrawn and for no apparent reason experiencing an ever-growing sense of isolation. Late in the Michaelmas Term in 1954 I went on my own volition to see Ireland's leading psychiatrist, Dr Norman Moore, at his consulting rooms in Fitzwilliam Street. He told me to find more outlets, and to come back the following year. I believe he thought that by studying too intensely I was jeopardising my health; I was too introverted and at that important point in my life I was not giving myself a fair chance. He told my parents that there could not possibly be anything seriously wrong with me when I was doing so well at university. (It was some time after this that he said to Brian that in a future age there would be the full answer to a problem like mine in 'the chemist's shop'.)

I had already started to hallucinate by 1954. The 'voices' I heard must have been a projection from my own mind of my understandably low opinion of myself into the spoken words of others. Thus these words, which I found insulting and provocative, were attributed by my unstable and alienated mind to the people about me.

I used to tell myself through my 'voices' that I was a homosexual, which was untrue and the antithesis of what I held myself to be, that I should soon die and that my loved ones would then laugh hilariously at their pejorative memories of me, before rapidly forgetting I had ever existed.

Rightly or wrongly, I believed at that time that it was the worst possible insult for a man to call one of his peers 'a homosexual'. That my hallucinations took that particular form could not have been more distressing for me, given the circumstances of my upbringing, the views of my family and my own nature. The psychotic wounds in my psyche went so deep as a result that even after I started to improve with more effective medication in January 1959, they were reopened if I suspected there was a homosexual around anywhere—near me in a pub, on the radio or television, or even simply the author of a book I had started.

My apparent bias came entirely from my psychosis. This caused me to adopt an inflexible attitude to a certain proclivity in human nature with which it has been difficult for me to come to terms.

In early 1955 I was studying at home in my bedroom on the ground floor, in the late afternoon, when I heard a knock at my door. I called out, 'Come in!' My parents used to have several staff working for them at Geragh. There, standing half-naked in the doorway of a house briefly empty apart from the two of us, was our teenage live-in maid from the country. She made as if to move to my bed, but I had to stop her. Something told me then that for some unaccountable reason I was going to be physically unable to have sex. The maid at Geragh was one of several girls I had fancied, but to no avail. Had I not met Nancy some four years later it is doubtful that I should ever have had an explicit sexual relationship, let alone one which endured for our first seven very happy years of marriage and produced a healthy son.

Within a short while my personality had totally disintegrated. I became incapable of responding to the things I had held dear, including close personal relationships. I could not understand what was happening to me. Nor could I fight against it. I believed I was about to die and, knowing my parents loved me very much and had always looked forward to a great future for me, I wanted to leave the best memory of myself that I could. No one else was as yet aware of this creeping mental and emotional paralysis.

I continued to study during every waking hour. We had no Economics examinations in the second year. In May 1955 I sat the First Year Law examinations. I recently acquired a copy of the results:

there were five subjects, and my average mark was seventy-eight per cent, including first place in two subjects. The Dean of the Law Faculty, Professor Patrick McGilligan, told my parents I was one of the most brilliant students he had known.

It has always been a source of mystification to me that no one, not my parents, my brothers, my doctors, my teachers or my fellow students, seems to have been aware of what had been happening to me between autumn 1953 and May 1956. Admittedly, however, to compensate for my alienation from myself I used to try to act as if I were normal, like any normal man from my own background. Having been quite good on the stage at Glenstal and, at first, at UCD, I used to summon up my thespian skills in given social situations, though to no avail from my point of view. If I succeeded in deceiving anyone it was because I was young and no one associated me with mental illness.

However, once during a party at Geragh my cousin asked her mother, my Aunt Betty, why I was standing in a corner, shifting from foot to foot in an extremely agitated manner. Betty explained that she thought I was very sick, probably with some sort of mental illness, and suggested that she look at my face, which was racked with pain, rather than my actions, conspicuous though they were. (Betty's daughter related this conversation to me years afterwards.) My tortured expression was the outward sign that my capacity to think and feel deeply had been replaced by gratuitous, uncontrollable and constant inward torment. First my personality and then my powers of concentration had fragmented.

At one point when I was going through my worst suffering, my mother came into my bedroom, where I was resting, to try and comfort me. She spoke to me as tenderly as if I were still a little child. However, because she had always been the person closest to my heart, at that stage she seemed like an extension of my pain. I howled like a wolf and she left quietly. My sister, Ciarín, then too small to be able to alert anyone else, remembers me crying out at the top of my voice in pain and terror on numerous occasions. Her bedroom and mine were on the ground floor, out of earshot of the rest of the family, and she would hear me howling in the night, alone and in despair.

The first time I was violent towards anyone else was when I attacked Brian at Geragh. My mother had sent him into the garage to fetch something and I was already busy in there. Suddenly, totally unprovoked and without warning, I went for him. Brian defended himself and in the middle of our fight my distraught mother appeared and called out repeatedly for me to stop. Brian then overpowered me and my violence came to an end. I was particularly sorry to have behaved in that way towards Brian and my mother. My actions were completely out of character and I cannot help wondering now if my violence was a kind of desperate cry for help.

My relationship with my mother had been a very close one. For the first twenty years of my life she meant everything to me: a nobler, more gentle, kinder and much more worthy version of myself. I loved to shine academically to please her and this had the bonus effect of pleasing my father. I saw pleasing my parents as doing my natural and agreeable duty and was particularly delighted if I could give pleasure to my mother in her own right, though, seeing them as one indivisible unit and revering my father as I did, it would not have meant nearly as much to me if I had not known that he was always there in the background. Very sadly, when I became gravely ill this relationship lost a great deal. What little was left of my consciously responsive emotional self made it difficult for me to respond to her affection for me, though the love she had for me lost none of its depth or tenderness. We saw a lot of one another be-tween the time that I returned home from Louvain and when I was hospitalised for the first time. I am told, though I am sorry to say I cannot remember, that we played golf together nearly every day at the golf clubs in either Killiney or Dún Laoghaire. I sensed in those years, albeit inarticulately as yet, that something unpleasant was happening to me and, like a badly wounded animal, I instinctively sought my mother's protection. Metaphorically speaking, I crawled back into the womb, as there it was easier to pretend there was no pain.

When I was studying for my Second Year Bachelor of Law ex-ams in 1956, I wrote in my diary, 'There I go again, screaming like a pig in the darkness of my sty'. My despair was due to my inability to cope with the relentlessly increasing alienation from my old self. In Freudian terms, it would seem to me that as by then there was no stable personality at all left to house my conscious intelligence, the latter, or my ego, became almost entirely subject to the whims of my libido and id. Considering how ill I was, and how much more so I was to become, I realise now that it was only with great diffi-culty that, aided by my earlier strong social conditioning at home and the discipline of over three years of Benedictine schooling, I was prevented throughout the forty worst years of my illness from behaving more badly than I actually did. I am also the more grate-ful, in the light of popular misconceptions about schizophrenia, that I never committed a crime. In my case, once I was on long-term medication, I generally tried because, I believe, of my inherent nature and my ingrained childhood spiritual faith, to do the right thing, though as my mentality had not developed since adolescence I could not always fully understand the reason why I did so.

In May I failed my Bachelor of Law exams. However, because

of my earlier showing, I had been elected to the King's Inns Students' Committee. Distinguished guest speakers, including Seán MacBride, sometime Minister of External Affairs and the founder of Amnesty International, were invited to our meetings.

The crisis came after I had failed my exams and before I was due to sit the Economics Finals, when I attacked my brother Michael and my father's driver-cum-handyman in the driveway at Geragh. Fortunately neither of them was hurt and I merely suffered a cut hand, which I had punched through a door in my efforts to get at Michael. My parents were then overseas on holiday. My mother's sister Betty, who was always very close to our parents and us, was staying in the house with us. Betty was a tender and loving person and had been extremely worried about me. She at once realised the implications. She took me upstairs and gently and without fear washed and bandaged my hand. It was one of the few acts of human kindness I was to experience for some time.

The family doctor was sent for and he learned that I had already been violent towards my brother Brian and now had attacked Michael. When the doctor discovered I was hearing 'voices' he realised that my aunt had been right to fear for my condition. He refused to drive me to the mental hospital himself. This was left to Brian.

St Patrick's Hospital in the centre of Dublin was founded in the 18th century by Jonathan Swift, the Dean of the nearby St Patrick's Cathedral. My feelings on finding myself there had the same character of inevitability as I had experienced before, first when I became an adolescent and then during my Architecture year at UCD when, a prey to pressures from all sides, I sensed the imminence of some devastating occurrence. Later on, in the summer of 1957 in London, I had the same feeling again, before my relapse. I felt like a helpless spectator at a play about the downfall of an ordinary young man. My powerless spirit was the spectator, unable to benefit from the catharsis usually experienced by an audience.

The hallucinatory 'voices' I projected into the spoken words of others reflected my self-punishing and cruel view of the impersonal colourless vacuum that had replaced my constantly longed-for but unattainable self of yesteryear. With my powers of concentration gone, seemingly forever, and my personality fragmented to the point of virtual non-existence, all that remained was a pure disembodied spirit in an otherwise empty physical frame, with which I was unable to do anything to help myself. Through some innately self-destructive urge, I constantly rounded on the impersonal colourless void which by then passed for my old self, and I projected on to my defenceless and vulnerable spirit my unjustifiably low opinion of this 'new' suffering and sick self; just as wolves might turn in a desperate and savage pack on an old and wounded wolf and tear him to pieces. However, in the end this disembodied pure spirit of mine remained unsullied and untouched by my illness. In a sense I can say that I was always able to call my soul my own, if only that; it was merely susceptible to pain, caused by my symptoms themselves. My own relentless and severely punishing opinion, criticisms and doubts about the inadequacies of my sick self invariably caused my spirit more suffering than did the adverse reactions of those who did not know me well.

When Brian drove me through the gateway of St Patrick's, down a slope towards a large grey stone building, I saw with a mixture of awful dread and philosophical resignation a massive uncompromising structure which gave me the impression of a primitive lack of human feeling and the sense that no patient was ever discharged alive. The picture I had of mental hospitals was the Hollywood version, looking back to those of the 1700s when the ever-compassionate Swift felt it necessary to build St Patrick's, and I had read that patients lay on stone floors covered with straw and were beaten when they cried out in anguish and manacled to the walls to prevent them from attacking anyone. In contrast, once I was admitted I found that the dormitories were clean and painted in pastel colours and that the nursing care in particular was excellent. Though the main building was at the foot of a slope, there was a lower level still, with the open-air recreation area and the Basement, which housed the incurable patients. In those days, such patients lived there literally until they died, as none of today's more effective treatments had been discovered.

The Basement consisted of a series of rooms without doors. It was dimly lit and had the original grey stone walls and floors of Swift's day. The patients shuffled round their rooms in cheap drab hospital clothes, with no apparent purpose in view except perhaps to keep moving, or else sat motionless on stone benches against the walls, with staring, vacant expressions. They had an exercise yard walled off from the rest of the patients, where their lives ebbed away in the same way. There was a patient down there who had been a brilliant engineer. He had been given a lobotomy operation and had turned into a soulless and mindless empty shell. Whenever I saw him he would repeat the same words parrot-fashion about having been an engineer, but they seemed to have no meaning for him. After speaking he would giggle mirthlessly, while his eyes remained totally blank. I was sent to deliver the milk to the Basement every day towards the end of my stay in St Patrick's and I now think that this was to remind me of what lay in store for me if I failed to cope with my disease. But when Brian drove me up to the front door, despite the bleak thoughts which chased through my mind, I had little idea of how nearly this was to become a reality a couple of years later.

In St Patrick's I was put on Largactil pills, then one of the most common forms of medication. Within a few weeks I stopped hearing 'voices' and generally became my old self. I made friends with another young patient, a Dubliner called Séamus Dunne. Séamus was known as 'Stinker' Dunne because of his liking for expensive aftershave. 'Stinker', a man about town, spent a lot of time telling me about the art of seduction. Though I was to remain a virgin for three more years I felt flattered to be given advice of that nature by a man who impressed me as something of an expert.

At this time I told my mother what I remembered of an incident which happened when I was very young and asked her how old I had been at the time. My memory was of being myself a toddler and Michael a baby in a pram. We lived in the top flat of a house near the centre of the south side of Merrion Square in Dublin, almost directly opposite what was later to be my father's office. We had a nanny in a starched uniform who used to carry Michael, myself and the pram up and down the steep stairs every day. She would often take us into Merrion Square park when the weather was fine. On this particular day the three of us were in our usual place at a shelter in the centre of the park. All the nannies sat in the shelter and chatted while the children who were old enough played on a diagonal path in front of the shelter. Suddenly a pony with its cart bolted away from some workmen in the north-west corner of the park. The pony raced up the path towards where some of us toddlers were playing. The other nannies snatched their children up and took them into the shelter. My nanny was not fast enough so I remained on the path. The pony's hooves went over me and the wheels passed on either side. My mother said she remembered the occasion and that I was about eighteen months old. A few years ago, I found in my parents' personal papers a letter dated 12 August 1936 from a friend, asking if their youngster had fully recovered from his accident in Merrion Square park. Today over sixty years on I still sometimes wonder if God himself had a hand in my narrow escape.

By Christmas 1956 I was ready to be discharged from St Patrick's as more or less cured, though I still had to take the Largactil for a time. In January 1957 I resat my Second Year Law exams and passed. I was then to do light study and start my Final Year in both Economics and Law in October.

In early summer 1957 I decided I wanted to go to England to earn some pocket money. The doctors and my parents tried hard to dissuade me but when my parents travelled overseas, I caught the ferry to Holyhead.

After working for a while on the North Wales coast, I travelled to London. There I worked in Battersea Fun Park, Selfridges staff canteen and the kitchens at the Dorchester Hotel.

Soon after my arrival in London I visited an old friend of my father's, Éamonn Andrews, then on the threshold of a career as a national celebrity on television. I wished to ask Éamonn for his advice on how to get into the world of the theatre as I had already been quite successful on the stage both at Glenstal and at UCD. My reason for changing from a career in law was simply my foreboding that something even more devastating than before was about to happen and like a fish wriggling on the end of a line I was trying desperately to escape while I could. While Éamonn's wife Gráinne was making us a cup of coffee, Éamonn tried to dissuade me by tactfully pointing out that my fingernails were dirty and that one of the essential prerequisites for the aspiring actor is a presentable personal appearance.

All this time I was seeing a psychiatrist at George's Hospital, by Hyde Park Corner. I already had a prescription for my Largactil from St Patrick's, but when this had run out there was some confusion between the two hospitals as to who should prescribe some more pills. I could feel myself becoming more and more alienated from reality and I remember the psychiatrist saying that he simply did not have the authority to give me a prescription. I sent progressively more urgent letters home; in one I wrote 'I HAVE NO MORE PILLS' and after my father died I found this letter among his personal papers. However, my parents were still not available to answer my increasingly desperate requests and as no one was able to resolve the difficulty, within a few months the Largactil left my system entirely, inflicting permanent damage on my fragile psyche.

In October, after his return home from holiday, my father rang me while he was on a short visit to London. He could tell on the phone that I was even more seriously ill than before. I had been lodging with a cheerful and kind couple called Fryer above their sweetshop in Crawford Place, off the Edgware Road, but had just moved around the corner to cheaper though much less congenial accommodation and was sharing a first-floor room with a fellow-Irishman. At about midnight my father and a friend of his, Dr Gerry Slattery, an Irish doctor who lived in London, opened the door and switched on the light. The other lodger was thoroughly startled, but my father made me get dressed and pack and I spent the night at Dr Slattery's house. The next day my father took me back to St Patrick's by aeroplane. The journey was one of utter heartbreak and desolation for us both. The 'voices' in my head had never seemed more terrifyingly real to me. These 'voices', apparently from the depths of my being, vitriolically attacked my manhood and everything else that made me what I was. It was as if I were keeping my finger on my 'self-destruct button' to punish my spirit for having let my real self sink so low.

According to the Severe Invalidity Pension I have been getting since 1985, I am eighty-five to ninety per cent disabled. I became so in 1957, during those few months in London.

When I was again in St Patrick's the doctors put me back on Largactil. However, this time it proved to be ineffective. The severe mental anguish which resulted stemmed mainly from my relentlessly self-punishing attitude towards what my true personality had become.

After my relapse, I hardly spoke to anyone. Asked a question by my doctor or a nurse, I could answer only with difficulty. Within myself my feelings were of bewilderment, hopelessness and of being totally at a loss, both in the hospital and on my weekend visits back home to Geragh. It was as if my soul had left my body and was floating above me, an unvoiced witness to my ongoing inevitable and ultimate downfall. My St Patrick's self was in total variance to the witty and articulate conversationalist that I had been throughout my teens. My appearance too had changed dramatically and my healthy good looks had disappeared forever.

As is the experience of most patients in mental hospitals, I was, during this stay and those which followed, well treated not only by doctors and nurses, as one might expect, but by my fellow patients.

I introduce this matter only to make the point that, on two or three occasions when I was an in-patient in a mental hospital, I saw some of the more ignorant and brutalised psychiatric nurses physically abuse some of the more elderly frail and mentally retarded patients. Also I occasionally saw fellow patients of mine attack others and sometimes even a male psychiatric nurse.

After the failure of the Largactil, I was given two courses of electric shock treatment. I disliked this form of treatment and remember feeling very frightened beforehand. The treatment had no beneficial effect. For each shock, we patients lay on beds and were given an injection to put us to sleep. Afterwards I felt low and depressed and had a headache. I felt as if it was somehow my own fault that I was no better.

On one occasion, while a group of us was waiting for our electric shocks, a newly arrived teenage patient walked up and asked what we were doing. On being informed, his face lit up with a beatific smile. With evident relish, he asked an elderly manic-depressive if he wished to know the story behind electric shock treatment. The elderly patient did not look enthusiastic but the new arrival was keen to air his knowledge. He told his captive audience that an American scientist in the 1930s had developed a stun gun for use on pigs. With a sly smile, he explained that pigs can sense when they are about to be slaughtered and the stun gun shock to their foreheads beforehand makes them more submissive. His voice rising to a shrill falsetto, the young man concluded by saying that stun gun shocks on pigs had been adapted for use on mental patients. He then walked slowly away into the next ward, clicking his tongue and shaking his head. In the distance we could faintly hear a voice calling, 'Time for your medication, Mr Sparrow'. An anorexic girl suddenly jumped up and shrieked, 'We are such stuff / As dreams are made on'. In an attempt to lighten the atmosphere, a young postnatal depressive woman smiled at the manic-depressive in what she obviously intended to be a reassuring way, but which actually looked grotesque. Reading her intentions and seeing her difficulties, the old gentleman tried to respond in a manner befitting his senior station but only managed a grunt and a grave smile.

When the electric shock treatment had no effect, they tried drugging me into a deep sleep. When I awoke the doctor would ask me to describe my dreams. On one occasion I dreamed I was at a party with my closest relations and friends. In the dream I had fully recovered and was celebrating the start of a highly successful career as a politician. I was extremely distressed when telling the doctor this as I could sense that there was not the faintest chance of this dream coming true, That treatment also was discontinued.

I was violent on a third and last occasion.

While waiting in a queue for lunch at St Patrick's Hospital I attacked a fellow patient, a stranger, standing in front of me. I believe that on this occasion I entertained the same thoughts, if they can be called thoughts, and the same feelings as I had earlier when I attacked Brian and then Michael and my father's handyman at Geragh. As before, I had hallucinated that the man had said something insulting about my manhood. (Perhaps because I am more an ear than an eye person my hallucinations were invariably aural.) The hallucinations I was driven to act on led me to think the people concerned, each a young man of about my age, had said something insulting of a sexual nature to a third party about me. None of my own personal feelings were involved. These seemed to have disappeared with the rest of my normal self, as I had once known it. I believe my old self had by then been replaced by impulses a cornered and wounded wild animal might display, within an empty human frame. My St Patrick's doctor, Dr Moore, told me my 'voices' came from my abnormally low self-esteem. I felt alienated from myself and from others, and it was not until more effective medication was prescribed for me in early 1959 that I became even vaguely aware of what others actually thought about me, even though it was still in a paranoid and thus exclusively cerebral and unfeeling way. My paranoid delusions of grandeur were unaffected by any consideration of other people.

On the three occasions when I was violent, and each time towards particularly kind and gentle young men, it was because I involuntarily made myself think, or hallucinated, that each had insulted me in, to my mind, the worst possible way, by saying I was a homosexual. I saw Brian, Michael and my fellow-patient as rivals, as a threat to my quest for a female partner. I was paranoically obsessed by my virginity and by a desperate need to prove myself, or what I by then wrongly saw as myself, with a girl. My virginity made me feel exposed to being thought a homosexual. In the case of Michael and my father's handyman, for example, I hallucinated that one had said something insulting about me to the other. Immediately, it was as if something exploded inside my head, and I was gripped by an uncontrollably strong urge to attack them with my fists, 'to teach them a lesson'. At that point I no longer saw them as two people I knew well and who were fond of me, as I was of them, but as strangers and sworn enemies.

My phobia about being thought a homosexual was to my mind intimately linked with what turned out to be my long-term virginity. Dr Moore asked me many times when he came on his rounds if I felt I was able to concentrate. This notion, though very relevant to my well-being, had by then lost its meaning for me and, instead of answering with a truthful negative, I always countered with my own question, one with which I was obsessed. Namely, when did he think I would be able to have sex with a girl for the first time. Though Dr Moore explained to me that this would happen when I met a girl and fell in love, I was too withdrawn into my own world for his words to mean anything.

As far as I was concerned, my relatively late virginity was clear evidence that I must after all be a latent homosexual. Deep in some subconscious corner of my mind may have been the idea that as my parents and their circle clearly thrived on their bohemian lifestyle, so there must be something very odd about me, whose lifestyle in sexual terms was non-existent. I saw my father's casual sexual attitude to attractive women as the norm for great men, though in explicit terms I was unaware of my parents' sexual adventures till some years after they had both died. When eventually I was told about them, my initial reaction was one of shock and disbelief. During their lives I had raised them both on to an extremely high intellectual and moral pedestal and, even after I had heard the truth about them, they each retained a foot on their respective pedestals as far as I was concerned.

In the spring of 1958 my parents took me to Lourdes. It was the centenary of the reputed apparitions and maybe they hoped for a much-needed miracle. My father got me to act as a *brancardier*, or stretcher bearer, meeting physically handicapped invalids from the trains. There may not have been a miracle in the accepted sense, but I believe that indirectly the visit was extremely beneficial.

In September 1958 when I was nearly twenty-five my father, faced with Dr Moore's decision that I was now incurable, sent me to England, to Fulbourn Hospital near Cambridge. As I was passing through London I was asked by my father's friend Dr Slattery, in whose house I had stayed the previous year, to call in at the Maudesley Institute. A Dr Carstairs examined me there and gave it as his opinion that my illness would eventually burn itself out. Many years later, I heard that some forty per cent of schizophrenics begin to improve when they are in their early fifties.

Fulbourn Hospital was built about a century later than St Patrick's, in the 1800s; the brickwork building was begrimed with age and made an equally forbidding impression on me when I arrived there. This hospital had been recommended to my father because of its brilliant young Medical Superintendent, Dr David Clark, whose advanced ideas for the treatment of patients had given Fulbourn a high success rate. As a young army doctor Dr Clark had visited Auschwitz after the War and had seen the depths of human degradation, suffering and despair at first hand. At this time Dr Clark was in his thirties, a clean-cut man who habitually wore a blazer and had a ready Pickwickian twinkle in his eye. He was lion-hearted in his willingness to help those for whom all hope had been abandoned. Though once I had settled down I found the nursing care less uniformly good than at St Patrick's, I was fortunate indeed to have been sent to what was, by universal consensus, the most advanced psychiatric hospital in the world.

Soon after my arrival at Fulbourn Hospital I was seen by a panel of doctors who were aware that I had been violent and I was at once transferred to a ward for incurables in the Victorian main building. Most of my fellow patients were elderly and went to bed in our dormitory after the four o'clock supper. The diet was Spartan. I was allowed out to the hospital shop and to visit a nearby public house of my choice in the evenings. Patients like myself had to be back in our ward by nine o'clock, when the door was locked for the night. This was a hard time, though even then the flame of hope did not entirely die within me; perhaps it was the optimism natural to youth.

Looking back, I remember with gratitude the selfless care given by one man who, unsung, spent his working life doing the often thankless job of trying to help people like myself back on their feet, when the world had turned its back on them. This was Doug Naylor, who was in charge of the Occupational Therapy Unit and who exemplified infinite patience and kindness. I was to meet him in Fulbourn again many years later.

The turning point

The illness very slowly, and like an invisible and insidious cancer, penetrated my personality through to the hard core of my capacity for personalised thought and self-conscious emotion. Over the worst years from 1957 to 1959 I was unrecognisable from my parents' viewpoint and also from my own. My appearance had altered, leaving me looking haggard and old and my former healthy self had become a longed-for but unattainable dream. I resembled a creature from an alien planet; to all intents and purposes I was a walking, talking automaton.

Although even in those dark years I would never have been driven to attack a child, my mother or any other female, or my father, a doctor, nurse, priest or anyone else in authority, I had lost control of my personality and my intellectual and emotional infrastructure had become a giant maelstrom of mental turmoil and pain. Any attempt to comfort me, particularly by my mother, simply caused more pain. My world had been turned inside out.

I felt that it was as if the Devil himself had been allowed access to my innermost being and had exchanged a fiery ball of inner chaos and torment for my soul, my consciousness of my self and my capacity for understanding. This was all the more devastating as it blocked any further development of my ability to understand my old self vis-à-vis my understanding of others.

Milton puts it well in *Paradise Lost*: 'The mind is its own place, and in itself / Can make a heav'n of hell, a hell of heav'n'.

3. Nancy

One particular evening sortie of mine from Fulbourn Hospital I shall remember for the rest of my days. On New Year's Day 1959, I left the Robin Hood in Cherry Hinton to walk the mile back to the hospital. A pretty woman, with short, well-groomed light-brown hair, wearing a pale-brown lambskin coat, was standing at the bus stop. Until then I had spoken to virtually no one but I found myself talking to her. She told me her name was Nancy. I learned that she also was a patient at Fulbourn Hospital, and that she was recovering from a nervous breakdown.

After this first encounter, Nancy and I met again and again and gradually formed a relationship which rendered us inseparable. Nancy was a slim, petite and attractive woman, intelligent in what was once described as a particularly intuitive way. We rapidly came to love one another unconditionally and deeply and for seven years our love never faltered.

She told me her nervous breakdown resulted from a divorce in which she had been the injured party, and that she had a six-year-old son. As therapy she helped at the hospital hairdresser's. She said she would be thirty-five on 19 January. I was twenty-five.

Nancy and I found we shared many interests, including a love of classical and popular music. One of my favourite songs after our first meeting, which now brings back tender memories, was 'Nancy with the laughing face'.

Nancy

Nancy told me that during the War she had worked in the Land Army on the rich black arable soil near her home in the small Cambridgeshire Fens market town of March. A little later in the War she had gone into domestic service in London with a barrister called Markham and his family. She met her first husband in March. He was ten years her senior and was subcontracted to the Post Office to repaint letter-boxes. Union rules prohibited females from working, so Nancy piled her hair under a cloth cap and dressed as a boy-apprentice to help her husband.

She had a sister, Louie, and a brother, Bill, to whom she was very attached, as she was to her parents and especially her father. Nancy was her parents' favourite child. Later in 1959 Nancy and I travelled from Fulbourn Hospital to March to attend Bill's wedding at the Catholic church. Sadly, Bill died that Christmas without knowing that his wife was carrying his son.

In the first few weeks of 1959 a new drug called Stelazine arrived on the market. It was one of the first of the so-called 'major' tranquillisers and Dr Clark prescribed it for me. It appeared eighteen months after I became severely disabled and five-and-a-half years after the first onset of my illness. In tandem with my newly formed relationship with Nancy the new drug was extremely beneficial. A little later Dr Moore told me it had arrived in the nick of time for me. Gradually the colourless, impersonal and haunted latter-day self of my illness became slightly less painful to me and I was less liable to suffer from the false accusations, obsessions and self-doubts of my spirit.

As a result of my gradual improvement, I was transferred back to one of the new wards separate from the main building.

In my Dublin days I had been of average-to-good standard on the Dublin tennis club circuit. In the early summer of 1959 the hospital games master challenged me to a match. The match was a hard-fought one and much to my surprise and pleasure I won. Nancy was delighted. At this time Nancy was pronounced fully fit, but was given Dr Clark's permission to remain for a few weeks at the hospital to be near me.

She was blessed with a noble and generous spirit that inclined her always towards helping the weak; this attracted me to her as I felt she was the only human being apart from my mother who could see in me more than an empty shell. Nancy and I spent every possible moment together. She spent many hours trying with a certain amount of success to achieve the 'medically impossible' task of unravelling the large number of 'knots' inside my head. From our many talks she was able to glean from my then usual slurred speech that I had had a good education. She was the first person to whom I had responded in over five years of illness and as there were signs that the newly available drug was going to offer me the chance of being able to salvage something of my education, she threw in her lot with mine. The move was against the advice of both families, but was encouraged by her own doctor, Dr Young, and by my doctor, Dr Clark.

For a time after we met, whenever our walks took us through the hospital vegetable gardens, I used to pull up carrots and eat them still covered with soil. I felt no sense of impropriety and I saw myself as a devil-may-care rake who could do anything; I knew I could get away with such behaviour.

In the summer of 1959 Nancy left the hospital to work as a live-in waitress at the Red Lion Hotel in Grantchester. She worked so conscientiously that the owners, Reg and Ann Fuller, soon came to rely on her more than they did on any of their other staff.

Nancy made me feel as though I was someone of worth once

more. Soon my physical desire to make love with her became very strong. Having failed to get anywhere with other girls before I met her, I now began to feel that maybe Dr Moore had been right when he said that my apparent impotency would resolve itself when I fell in love. Also I sensed that Nancy was falling in love with me. For months I was like a hunter on the trail of his quarry. In the autumn she gave way to my advances. The episode was eventually to prove the definitive meeting-point of our two paths. Not long beforehand my 'voices' had been telling me I was a damned soul who would soon die and be happier in Hell than alive.

Whatever else went through my mind before our lovemaking, I also experienced a new sense of personal life-enhancement and a profound sense of gratitude that anyone, let alone someone of Nancy's calibre, should care to such an extent for someone like myself. I think I knew too that as I was so shy of girls and had always immersed myself in study and sport to the exclusion of everything else, Nancy would be my first and probably only girlfriend. Being too withdrawn to make any overtures, I had up till that moment restricted myself to admiring many attractive girls of my age secretly.

I have one memory of my diffidence which dates back to the earliest days of my illness, to Christmas 1955. A fellow Law student, Anthony Devitt, and I had driven down to County Wicklow to a party at the house of a friend of his. There was one particularly attractive girl at the party. I was too shy to speak to her and doubt if she was even aware of me. Anthony and I had to leave the party early for the long drive back to Dublin and when we were about twenty yards down the drive I hallucinated that the girl screamed out of the window, 'I can't stand the bugger', referring to me.

At the time the hallucination, for that will have been what it was, seemed very real and it left me, I remember, deeply distressed, but now my relationship with Nancy began to give me a new perspective and an opportunity, for a while, to set aside some of my inhibitions.

I had been sent out regularly from the hospital since the summer of 1959, to see if I could hold down a relatively undemanding job in a local laundry. I had already worked in the hospital laundry where, I must admit, my performance left a lot to be desired. The reason was that I was unable to concentrate for any length of time, and the resultant catatonic mental trance left me without vitality or motivation. However, I believe that in arranging jobs for me Dr Clark was clutching at the straw of evidence that the Stelazine medication together with my relationship with Nancy was having a good effect. My father, so keen for my sake that I should be fit to return to the fold in Dublin, was also encouraged by the same signs and when visiting me on one occasion he took a crate of vintage wine to Dr Clark to express his thanks.

While I was earning my first real wages an elderly fellow-patient from the hospital noticed my trance-like state and warned me to 'buck my ideas up' or I would be in trouble. In the event, I was dismissed sometime in August because I had withdrawn into my own world too much to do a good job. Dr Clark soon found me a third chance of holding down employment, in a laundry in another part of Cambridge. From autumn 1959 I worked in the laundry room of Mill Road Maternity Hospital.

I was allowed to return home to Geragh for Christmas in 1959. While there I visited the Dean of the Law Faculty. He said that as I had passed the Second Year exams in the Law Degree course at the resit in January 1957 it would be possible for me to go back and do my Final Year.

Nancy

After my holiday I returned to Fulbourn Hospital armed with this information. When I saw Nancy, she told me with some alarm that she was pregnant. This was unexpected as both she and I thought we had taken the necessary precautions.

There had never been anyone like Nancy in my life and she had become and remained very dear to me. However, the thought of having to get married alarmed me; I was not ready to marry anyone at that point. Encouraged by my parents, who were yet to learn how vital Nancy was to my welfare, I entertained hopelessly unrealistic ideas of returning to my Law studies and of becoming a barrister. Nancy, on the other hand, lived a restricted life with her frail and elderly parents and her young son in a small two-bedroom semi, where later, in 1960, they would be joined by Nancy's widowed sister-in-law and her baby. My father suggested the child I had fathered might be adopted but, to avoid a relapse for Nancy, Dr Clark and Dr Ruth Young, Nancy's doctor and a personal friend, advised an abortion. Nancy was distraught and at first uncomprehending; the man she had come to look upon as her right arm had at our first big test turned out to be feckless and unreliable. After the abortion she came to understand and accept that, despite her own commitment to our future together and my encouraging reaction to the new medication, my illness was too severe for me to be able to help, except to a limited extent.

Our baby was aborted in the maternity hospital where I worked in January 1960. I visited Nancy every day in what was known as 'Heartbreak Ward'. We learned that the baby would have been a perfectly formed little girl. The abortion put a heavy strain on Nancy. Sadly, for obvious reasons, she had suffered more than most prospective mothers did vis-à-vis their partners. She always found it too painful to speak about our baby at any length, though she never forgot her. Alone now, I shall remember Jennifer, our daughter who never was, for the rest of my life.

Somehow I managed to hold down my laundry job at Mill Road Maternity Hospital for longer than the minimum three months stipulated by Dr Clark as necessary to show that, were he finally to discharge me, I should not be totally unable to cope. I then got work as a storekeeper at a firm making agricultural machinery called Dorman Sprayer. This was owned by a Mr Dorman, a mild, likeable man with prematurely white hair, whose accent told me he had originally come from Northern Ireland. There is no doubt that Nancy's presence in my life helped me as again I coped reasonably well with this job for about three months.

I should add that throughout the period between the summer of 1959 and October 1960, I made rather more unsuccessful than successful attempts to keep a job. Included in the former were the first two laundry jobs, a job in the despatch department at Pye's factory, a window-cleaning job and work as a cleaner in the students' dining-hall at one of the Cambridge colleges. Also towards the end of this period, I trained to be a vacuum cleaner salesman living on commission alone. For two or three weeks I had some near-sales and impressed my employer. But this work is daunting even for most normal men and I left without making a sale. I used to consider my vacuum cleaner salesman experiences to be a case for saying, 'The operation was a success but the patient died'.

The abortion only served to bring Nancy and myself even closer together. Every evening I cycled the three or four miles each way to visit Nancy. On one occasion I bought some vermilion lace lingerie for her from a leading Cambridge store. Looking back, I can see that the present was in poor aesthetic taste but as she convinced me she was pleased, I felt very happy. I suppose I must for many years have given most people, if not Nancy or my mother, the impression of being like a backward overgrown schoolboy for whom every day was a holiday.

I remember clearly my days in Grantchester and Cambridge. They were days of excitement and fun for Nancy and me. We sometimes picnicked at a well-known beauty spot on the Cam near Grantchester, or took tea with home-made bread and jam in an orchard tea-garden. During the summers of 1959 and 1960 we went to the Fair in Cambridge on Midsummer Common and punted on the Cam, or cycled or walked to Jesus Green swimming pool. On the strength of my earlier swimming ability I sometimes felt confident enough to lead Nancy in our own improvised lovers' water ballet. My amateur aquatic efforts were beautiful to us though I dread to think how they may have appeared to the other swimmers.

We also had the opportunity of attending the Cambridge University undergraduates' May Balls. Nancy had a ball-gown given to her by her former husband. The gown was of blue, brown and gold with a motif of pansies. I liked to see her wear it, especially when we were dancing together, and was glad she always kept it. I took Nancy up to London by train from Cambridge on two or three occasions. On one trip we visited my aunt, Betty, who was living there then. Betty and Nancy struck up an immediate and lasting rapport. Much of the reason for their affinity may have been that they were both divorcees who had suffered at the hands of the men in their lives and both, at least as far as Nancy was concerned at this early stage, had since met more suitable partners.

Our fun days continued apace. In the early years Nancy, a bright new light in my life, personified all my hopes for the future. Perhaps I had the same effect on her. Our pleasure in one another's company was based on Nancy's conviction that she could, with the help of the medication and her love and care, cure me to the extent that I would be able to lead a normal life and enjoy a professional man's career. I basked in the sunshine of her belief and became myself optimistic about my future.

In August 1960 I took Nancy by ferry from Holyhead to Dún Laoghaire. To save a taxi fare we walked the mile to Geragh. After a day or two, my father and a friend of the family, driven by my father's chauffeur, went with my brothers Brian and Niall and Nancy and myself down to my father's cottage on Kenmare Bay in County Kerry. Things started out well; Nancy and I went for long walks beside the sea on my father's land and all of us played poker in the evenings. Then one evening, still encouraged by the signs of slight improvement that I had shown in England, my father took me aside and strongly advised me to break with Nancy. He said that because she and I did not have enough in common we should both sooner or later be unhappy were we together. The following morning my father asked me to do a small job on his land. When I returned there was no sign of Nancy. I learned that my father had asked his driver to take her to Kenmare Railway Station to catch the Dublin train. Later I was told that one of my father's partners had met her in Dublin and driven her to the Dún Laoghaire ferry.

Shortly after finding that Nancy had left, I was given a note from her by the family friend, who said she had come across it under a Bible on my pillow. In the note Nancy asked me not to desert her, for my own sake as well as because she was in love with me. I felt confused and was torn between the desire to try hard for my father's sake to forget Nancy and concentrate on my future, and my natural inclination to be with the one person who seemed to understand me and wanted to share my life.

A few days later I was back in Cambridge. By this time I was living at a rehabilitation hostel in Lensfield Road, called Winston House. I still had my father's advice ringing in my ears, but I soon began to miss the good times I had been having with Nancy. Also, though I was too withdrawn to understand the situation fully, I was vaguely aware that there would probably never be anyone else with whom I could share such times.

After a few days of uncertainty I rang Nancy at the Red Lion Hotel and she told me she was again pregnant; she used to joke later that I only had to look at her and she would conceive. This news made me even more confused, but I began to believe that I should stay with her and that we probably needed each other.

So Nancy and I were reconciled. She repeatedly suggested to me that we get married and on one occasion added that if we did not, she would have to have another abortion. I could accept the justice of this and I had to admit to myself that, though it is true that one of the symptoms of my illness is religious mania, I nevertheless felt certain that the feeling I now had, based on what I had been taught in my strict Christian upbringing, was founded on an absolute truth—that is to say, that abortion amounted to murder. I knew I could not allow a baby of ours to be aborted again.

There would be family opposition, though. I had met Nancy's father two or three times when she and I visited her home. He felt strongly that if Nancy and I were married, it would sooner or later make his daughter unhappy. I already knew my own father's views. Basically I felt the same as when I had fathered my first child: I was not ready for marriage, but this time I felt I had no choice.

In September 1960 I was on the point of running away to my parents in Ireland in my anxiety and I confided in Mr Dorman's secretary. She knew that by then Nancy and I had made the decision to get married the following month and appreciated that my need for Nancy was vital to my welfare. Luckily for us both, she talked me round and persuaded me to stay.

I also asked Dr Clark for his advice and he said that, if he were in my place, he would marry Nancy.

Originally he had been opposed to the idea of Nancy and myself getting married. During her first pregnancy in early 1960, Nancy had said to me that if we did not get married I would 'miss the bus'. When I quoted her to Dr Clark he had replied, 'Don't worry; there's always another bus coming along.' His U-turn may have been prompted partly by my less than adequate attempts to prove myself employable, and partly by my self-evident dependence on her. He now asked me if I wished to be my father's hanger-on all my life. I suppose he may have wondered what alternatives there were for Nancy or myself at that point.

Nancy and I were married in the Catholic church on Hills Road, Cambridge on 17 October 1960. Nancy's mother and sister-in-law were present and also an uncle and aunt of hers. Her father was not there, so Nancy's uncle gave her away. There were two or three Cambridge friends of Nancy's and mine in the congregation and my parents were there together with my brother Michael, who was best man, and my young sister Ciarín.

After the wedding my father paid for a reception at one of Cambridge's leading hotels, the Garden House Hotel. Before everyone left, my father gave me enough money to cover a week's honeymoon. We stayed with a friendly couple called Mr and Mrs Doggett in their guest house beside a pub, near one of the old bridges over the Cam.

I expect Dr Clark had told my father that for me to marry Nancy at this stage was my best and last chance of remaining outside a hospital. I'm in no doubt that I was always in some ways merely infatuated with Nancy. As the years rolled by, my infatuation showed itself more and more to be unhealthy, and also I felt more and more inadequate. In turn this began to have an unhealthy effect on her morale and mine. However, in the early days she was my salvation.

After the honeymoon we went to live with Nancy's parents, her small son Laurence, and her sister-in-law and her baby, in their little house at 2 Peas Hill Road, March. As there was only one small kitchen table, we staggered our meals. One evening soon after our arrival, while Nancy and I were eating supper my father-in-law was watching my eating habits with growing disbelief and horror. Nancy leapt into action to protect me from feeling ostracised and told her father that he must understand that I could not help myself; as far as she was concerned, just because my table manners were clumsy owing to the difficulty I had in controlling my movements, it did not necessarily mean that I was totally unworthy of her. She pointed out that I was her responsibility and not his. Though Nancy had a deep and lifelong affinity with her father, he, unlike his wife, was never fully able to accept me.

4. Job success

In January 1961, at a time of full employment, I managed to get a job as a bus conductor based in March, in Cambridgeshire. The Personnel Officer at Branch H.Q. in Peterborough told me he would give me the job 'on face value'. This was encouraging for, as I grew older, my illness seemed to become more apparent. I remember that, like the other five new bus conductors, I was given two changes of summer and winter uniform, and a greatcoat for winter. The staff number on my lapel badge was 137.

Our son was born on 30 April 1961. I went with Nancy in the ambulance to a maternity hospital in nearby Wisbech. While Nancy sat in front beside the driver, talking and laughing light-heartedly, I remained in the back being sick. Deep inside I was overcome by the significance of the event.

At his birth the baby was thirteen inches long. As the umbilical cord had almost strangled him, he was put into an oxygen tent at first. Nancy's labour lasted for fifty-four hours and, as she had already had forty-eight hours labour with my stepson some years earlier, she was advised to have no more children.

We named our son Michael Seán after my father, who was called Michael John. Seán is the Irish for John and this was the name we always used. In June 1961 my father-in-law arranged for Nancy, our baby and myself to move into a semi-detached three-bedroom council house in Eastwood Avenue. We were joined temporarily by Nancy's sister-in-law and her baby. Our council house, Number 56, opposite Eastwood Cemetery gates, was the first of five comfortable homes that Nancy created single-handedly from the bare bricks and mortar. Because of my disability, Nancy's first son Laurence remained with his grandparents at Peas Hill Road.

Especially after Seán was born, I became afraid I would be dismissed from my job. Like the other bus conductors, I worked through all my holidays, including summer holidays, to make up my income. Only the law of the land prohibited us from working on Christmas Day. Every day was a formidable challenge. The strong drugs I was taking caused clumsiness and poor coordination, which made life difficult for me. At the end of the day, when I was counting my takings in the staff room, all the coins in the money satchel around my shoulder would sometimes spill all over the floor.

On a few occasions when I overslept for an early shift, my driver, George Wheeler, drove his double-decker bus to my house and hooted on the horn. I would then dress rapidly and put my cycle on the back of the bus. We would drive away at speed and, once I had deposited my cycle, take our passengers on board. Such goings-on had never been seen in Eastwood Avenue and I suspect they were talked about for some time. Some other close escapes from losing my job spring to mind. One afternoon George and I were in our bus at the terminus, about to cover one of the March town routes. Near the time for our departure, I felt called upon to relieve myself. I did this with all possible haste in a public house across the road. On my return I was surprised to see my bus driving away round the corner. When George returned in due course, I asked him why he had not waited for me to ring the bell before setting out. He answered that he had naturally assumed I was on board and that I had been lucky for, as it was early-closing day, he had picked up no passengers on either the outward or the homeward journeys. As the incident passed unnoticed by our local inspector-in-charge, George and I could afford to laugh about it.

On another occasion George and I were working our double-decker through the busy streets of Peterborough. We had nearly a full load when I allowed the last passenger on board with a lady who was obviously his wife. The gentleman was clearly a former military man with erect bearing, a short haircut, a bristling moustache, a regimental tie and a foot swathed in bandages. As we were late, George was driving at full speed. I was going up the aisle in the lurching bus asking for fares when suddenly I found myself treading on something large and soft, and heard a sharp yell. I turned around and saw with horror that I had trodden on the man's bandaged foot. Almost speechless with rage, the gentleman in question gasped out several profanities before exploding with, 'You incompetent dolt! You're an affront to your profession, sir!' I managed with extreme difficulty to placate him. When I had turned around at the front of the bus and was with difficulty making my uncoordinated way slowly back to the platform, I heard another yell very similar to the first. This time he refused to accept my even more profuse apologies. Still white with passion, he hurried off the bus at the next stop followed by his wife, taking my badge number and assuring me I had not heard the last of the matter. As the bus gathered speed again, I saw him at the stop shaking his fist and heard a faint angry shout. However, despite my worst forebodings I heard no more about the matter.

There were various other little episodes in those early days in March which reinforced my new and acutely unhealthy feelings of worthlessness. Though George generously covered for me when things went wrong, he said to me on one occasion that I was 'the rummest cove ever to work at the March depot'. He added rather unkindly that I need not think I was important; if I were to die, no one would miss me. Whereas a normal man would probably have laughed off such a remark, I was, for a brief moment, shocked out of the delusions of grandeur of my paranoid world. However, my illness was too severe for me to be able to face the rigours of everyday reality for long and I soon slipped back into my impossible dreams. Another time George advised me more gently to live my life as it truly was and to forget about what might have been or what might be in the future in some hypothetical world of my own. I wish I could have followed his advice, but I could not. It was as if I had imprisoned myself in a windowless, soundproof prison cell. I was in a world in limbo without day or night or seasons of the year, where I had lost all consciousness of my real self and could no longer relate to anyone, even people to whom I had once been close. This was a dead world in which, as if driven by fate, I had deprived myself of normal feelings and the voice to express them. When George and many others tried to help me, their words fell on deaf ears, for I was in a permanent state of suspended animation. Once George, exasperated about my attitude to one of my duties, said 'Are you a man or a mouse?' The fact that my reply was 'Well, I like cheese' indicates, I suppose, that my sense of humour had not deserted me, but also that, though the Stelazine made it possible for me to cope well as a busman for several years, it did not stiffen my resolve to the extent that I could assert myself. Indeed, there was nothing left to assert. My personality had been fragmented long before and I was capable of responding to an unfavourable situation only by being totally passive. Fortunately, the fact that I was born with a fairly resilient personality and that my character had been well formed helped me greatly, in combination with the medication and Nancy's great strength.

My inability to assert myself was incomprehensible even to those closest to me. It strengthened the general impression that people could treat me just as they wished. Matters did not improve much over time, for years later, when he was grown up, my son, Seán, was still telling me to stop being a 'mental spastic'. Like an overgrown and helplessly irresponsible adolescent, I could do nothing about being totally dependent on the goodwill of others.

While I was working as a bus conductor, Nancy used to work on the local arable farms. Before going to work, she would mount young Seán on her crossbar and cycle the mile to Peas Hill Road, where my mother-in-law looked after him. The hard winter of 1963 made particularly severe demands on her.

Once, in order to get a taste of a busman's job from the passenger's point of view, Nancy deposited our son with her mother, paid her fare and joined a double-decker load of holidaymakers I was taking to Skegness for the day. On our arrival she and I separated from the others and enjoyed the sights and amused ourselves in the way people usually do at a seaside resort.

When we were approaching March again, she borrowed my peaked hat and went upstairs and downstairs collecting contributions for the driver and myself. It greatly pleased me to see her enjoying the day out and being ready, as ever, to assert herself on my behalf. I was endlessly grateful for the mystery of our love and it had become the only encouragement I needed.

During our Eastwood Avenue days, we had plenty of visitors. May and Hilda came and afterwards they referred to Nancy in a letter as 'a great little home builder'. Brian visited us and so did Ciarín. My father came and stayed at the George Inn in the High Street. Soon after Nancy and I were married, I had asked my father for financial help but he replied that he could not afford to keep two families. Even with both our incomes and myself working every possible hour of overtime without a holiday, Nancy and I were poorer then than we would ever be again. But we would never again be as content.

In the winter of 1963, our heating went on the blink and I asked my father if he could use his influence to help. After a few days, we got a telegram saying a Mr X would be visiting us the next day to see to our heating. We expected a plumber and were suitably impressed when a new Daimler drew up outside. My father had rung a friend, the chairman of a domestic heating empire, merely saying his son and daughter-in-law would like to meet him. Our guest spent half-an-hour munching through Nancy's home-made bread and cakes before devouring a roast joint of prime beef that Nancy had saved for my birthday the next day. He then drank an entire bottle of vintage claret that my father had given us, settled back and spoke at length on how he had climbed his way to the top of the tree from obscure beginnings. Asked about our heating he looked pained, as if his aesthetic sensibilities had been dealt a severe blow, and indicated that he personally did not deal with such matters. With a quiver of irritation, he suggested that we ask a plumber a question like that, and definitely not a man in his position. He struck us as being pleased with himself as he said his goodbyes and as he was on his way down the garden path, we heard a discreet belch of gratification. We did not see or hear from him again. Happily, my father-in-law saved the day when he arrived soon afterwards with a good second-hand paraffin heater.

Once we got a telegram saying my father was on a whistle-stop tour of the area and that he would drive over and take Nancy and myself out to lunch. Nancy bought some good second-hand clothes for us both at a jumble sale and on the appointed day we awaited my father. As my father was rarely on time for his appointments, we were surprised to hear the purr of a car approaching, on time, around the Bullring, as the Eastwood Avenue estate is known. We were still more surprised when a Rolls-Royce driven by a liveried chauffeur drew up outside. The chauffeur rang the bell and asked if we were Mr and Mrs Anthony Scott. On being told we were, he said he had instructions to drive us to Walston Hall near Cambridge for lunch. He added that we were to be the guests of Lord and Lady Walston and that my father would be present to introduce us. As we were driving round the Bullring, Nancy laughed and whispered to me that she had never seen so many net curtains being twitched at once.

When, after an hour's drive, the chauffeur opened the door of the car for us, my father emerged to greet us with a broad smile and a glass of champagne for each of us.

In the spacious hall my father introduced us to Lord and Lady Walston, mentioning in an aside to us that Lord Walston was a Liberal peer who had defected to Labour and had once organised an African tour for the Queen, and that Lady Walston was a patron of the Arts, which was something that very much interested my father. A great friend of my father's, Father Dónal O'Sullivan SJ, like him, on the Irish Arts Council, greeted us warmly and invited me to follow his example and pour myself a pint of draught Guinness from a tap in the hall.

While we were in the drawing-room before lunch Lord Walston and Nancy had a lengthy conversation about politics, finding, as Nancy delightedly told me later, that many of their views coincided. I sat on a sofa beside my father, and as he and Lady Walston talked about a forthcoming art exhibition, enjoyed my pint in a pleasantly trance-like state.

A butler, two footmen and an under-footman served us at lunch, which consisted of several courses. Nancy was particularly impressed by the silver service. Afterwards we were driven home by the chauffeur once more, before the incredulous gaze of our neighbours.

My mother had a more philosophical attitude than my father towards the relationship between Nancy and myself, though on one occasion she asked me if I intended to remain a bus conductor all my life. She always wanted the best for me and believed I could still succeed in a more intellectual job. Years later, when she must have realised the intractability of my condition, she suggested I return to my old job on the buses, but by then there were only one-man operated buses in March.

Once when she was staying with us we had a near-tragedy at No. 56 on the night before she left for Dublin. Nancy's sister-in-law and her baby were in our second bedroom, my mother was in the spare bedroom and Nancy, baby Seán and I were in our bedroom. I had switched off our light when there was the sound of a bump from the spare room. Nancy thought my mother had dropped her book. Some deep-seated instinct told me something was wrong. I went into the spare room and saw the bedclothes were alight, the room was filled with smoke and my mother was lying unconscious on the floor. I dragged her out on to the landing and after a while she came round. She told us she had been reading her book and smoking a cigarette when she fell asleep. Happily she made a speedy and full recovery. I'm so pleased to have saved her life and that of everyone else by my unusually quick thinking.

Early in my busman's career a friend of my mother-in-law's, Alec Upton, had asked her who was the scruffy-looking fellow with the posh accent. Though Alec's question makes me laugh now, at the time it brought sharply into focus how my life had changed from being that of one of the best students of my generation in Dublin to that of a rather seedy, not to say potty, country bus conductor in England. Nevertheless, looking back I'm extremely proud that of the six of us who started together as conductors, I soon acquired the reputation of being the fastest at taking fares.

Despite my daily forebodings, I kept my busman's job for four and a half years, until I left to train as a teacher in September 1965. Today, when I consider the severity of my disability and my many attempts to prove myself independent of the State, I see my bus-conducting experience as an unqualified success.

5. Learning to teach

At this point in my life Dr Clark wanted me to take up teaching as the best way to use the education I had received. Over the previous four years, whenever Nancy had asked me if I would apply for a teacher-training college place, I used to say I was not ready to do so yet. On the one hand, I was vaguely aware my handicap was so severe that I would have little chance of being able to cope with a classroom full of lively young people. By early 1963 I also felt that, if I continued to work as a bus conductor with total conscientiousness and commitment, I could probably hold down the job for life.

However, in early 1965, spurred on by the encouragement of others, I applied at the age of thirty-one for a place at Culham College of Education at Abingdon, near Oxford. I hitchhiked over there on being granted an interview. The College turned out to be a staunchly Protestant institution. It is easily possible that the interviewing panel thought I did not look like teacher material anyway and when they said they thought I would be happier at a Catholic college, I panicked and told them that I certainly would not! That was the end of the interview and I returned sadly to March. I felt for a while that no college at all would have me, but eventually I took the suggestion of the Culham panel to heart and did some research in the local lending library on Catholic colleges of education in England and Wales. I found there was one college in London, and another in Manchester, run by the Christian Brothers and called De La Salle College. I applied for a place there and was granted an interview in London with the Principal, Brother Augustine.

Brother Augustine was a strict disciplinarian, who would stand for no nonsense from anyone. He reminded me in some ways of my old Benedictine Headmaster, Father Matthew Dillon, the Bear. Whereas with Father Matthew the strap had been the ultimate deterrent, with Brother Augustine it was, I later heard, summary and permanent rustication. There was a strong physical resemblance between the two men. In both cases, students understood that neither Head would balk at asserting his authority.

At the start of the interview Brother Augustine appeared pleased when quoting my letter saying I was interested in a Catholic college. When he said he would offer me a place at the college in Manchester, to start in the September, I was light-headed with delight. As I was leaving I said, 'I won't let you down.' He replied drily, 'You won't get the chance, Mr Scott.'

At the end of August I handed in my resignation as a busman. One evening just before I left, two policemen dropped into the staff room when I was alone, counting my takings and checking the total with my waybill. One of them began to belittle my intelligence until the other said he had heard from a bus driver that I was about to leave to do a course of study.

I had various comments from the other busmen. One of the drivers, Bob Unwin, who was also our TGWU representative, admitted that teaching was a better job than bus conducting. Bob did not express any thoughts he may have had about my chances of success. Another driver reminded me, 'There's many a slip 'twixt cup and lip'. A third pointed out that better men than I had failed to be teachers. With the benefit of hindsight I can appreciate that each man's opinion had some truth in it.

When I rang De La Salle College from the public phone-box in Eastwood Avenue and, somewhat apologetically, explained to the Bursar, Brother Thomas, that I had completed four and a half years as a bus conductor, he said, to my surprise, 'That's probably a good thing'. Today I realise that the Christian Brothers were probably aware of my schizophrenia, which was by then self-evident, from the outset. I imagine they took me on board because of my character references and academic record.

After I left my job on the buses, Nancy, four-year-old Seán and I went by train to Manchester and then by plane to Dublin for a holiday. At Crewe the train stopped for several minutes. People were still getting on and off the train when we noticed Seán was missing. Nancy looked through the window and saw him on the platform, looking lost. The guard's whistle blew as I jumped off the train and grabbed him. The train was already moving as I jumped aboard with him in my arms and closed the carriage door behind us both.

On the plane Seán sat beside Nancy and I was across the aisle. When the captain announced we were approaching Dublin Airport, young Seán, who could not understand how the plane could descend from the clouds to land without crashing, tugged at Nancy's sleeve and asked her if he could possibly borrow my parachute!

The visit to my family in Ireland was a happier one than that of five years before. My father seemed to have accepted my marriage to Nancy and was proud of my child as his first-born grandchild.

When we arrived back in Manchester from Dublin, Nancy and Seán went back home and left me to start my course. I had nowhere to stay and I eventually spent the first night in a Salvation Army hostel. The next day I found accommodation in a students' hostel attached to De La Salle in Cheetham Hill, Salford. I lived there for my first two terms.

At the students' hostel I found myself sharing a room with another mature student, Paul O'Rourke. Paul befriended me and was highly supportive throughout our time at college. As we both came into the mature student category we were expected to do the course in two rather than the usual three years. I was reading for a Teachers' Certificate in Combined French and English. Throughout the two-year course, though I seldom shone in the English coursework, I was regularly first in the class in the French coursework. The Head of the French Department, who was also the Vice-Principal, took a special interest in me. Brother Vincent Fleming was a charming and cheerful man, who told me he had got his degree from my old stamping-ground, UCD. Once, early on, when the two of us were discussing a seventeenth-century French play, he congratulated me for being 'on the right wavelength', which I found very encouraging.

Like Brother Thomas, Brother Vincent and the other Christian Brothers, Paul may also have guessed about my schizophrenia. Thankfully, no one at De La Salle considered it to be of primary importance; at the time, though, I was convinced no one was aware of it and took great steps to avoid it being evident. I realise today I was like an ostrich burying its head in the sand.

The stress levels I experienced at the College soon led to nervous tension, which caused involuntary neck movements. These consisted in my being unable to keep my head in a normal position if I was out anywhere. My head would turn upwards, or upwards and sideways, whenever I was away from home. I found the movements acutely embarrassing and they were to last for some twelve years. I was powerless to prevent them.

Soon after our arrival at the College all First Year students were required to undergo a medical examination. The brusque examining doctor told me that anyone who needed Stelazine medication was not fit to be a teacher. Without informing anyone I threw away my pills. When eventually I told Nancy the story in a letter, she became justifiably alarmed and took immediate steps to ensure I took my pills again. She no doubt remembered that once, while I was a bus conductor, I had thrown my bottle of pills into the River Nene in March. I had never suffered greatly from side effects; it was my dependence on the medication that I resented.

I continued to shine in my French coursework. At the end of an essay on Molière's *Tartuffe*, after he had written several superlatives, Brother Vincent wrote 'Olé!' in the margin.

Midway through the first term we had our first teaching practice. We went in a coach with a tutor from the hostel to another part of Salford. The children were young juniors. It turned out to be one of the few classroom experiences I enjoyed. Afterwards an impressed, but surprised, Paul told me that up to then he had not thought I had 'the necessary mental equipment' to be a teacher.

I was being trained to teach both secondary and junior children. I found the teaching practices a great strain, especially those in secondary schools. My over-anxious expectations of myself as a soon-to-be-qualified teacher were increased by the fact I knew the Christian Brothers expected the best of me as well. Early on in my career at De La Salle Brother Thomas had taken me aside and said that, as I was a mature student, I would be expected 'to raise the tone' of the College. This was an added anxiety for me.

Also I was aware that while my nineteen- and twenty-year-old fellow-students were capable of maintaining classroom order without difficulty, the same could not be said of me. While I always firmly intended to hold the children's attention by my 'authoritative presence' and thereby teach them along the lines of my written class-preparations, I knew each time in my heart of hearts that the situation ahead of me would most probably result in near-chaos like many had done before. If I had a strength as a teacher trainee it was in abstract, academic thought only. My inability to apply this practically was, and remained, as total as it had been in 1957 when I was first crippled.

The difficulty was not that my IQ was too low or that I did not have sufficient knowledge, but rather that, though the Stelazine had made it possible for me to 'get by', it was not, and indeed still is not, quite efficacious enough to give total release from the illness. And, of course, the children took advantage. My appearance was against me too. I looked strange and people often found me alarming and would take refuge in belittling me.

During the first term at De La Salle when I was beginning to concentrate on my studies after my ten-year break, I started to sense with inarticulate despair that Nancy and I did not have enough in common for us to bring out the best in one another over a lifetime, though at the time I was far too withdrawn from reality to be consciously aware of the problem. Somewhere deep inside, I sensed I needed a Nancy who, in addition to being a constant supporter and helpmeet, was also my spiritual and cultural soul mate, able to inspire me to surpass myself when required. My parents, and especially my father, had foreseen this would be the case and had warned me of the dangers, but in vain. My resultant uncomprehending and numb sense of sadness and loss lasted for the rest of Nancy's life and for several years after her death.

Around this time I also started to have a recurring daytime nightmare about Nancy and myself. Having been with May and Hilda to the Aran Islands in Galway Bay a couple of times as a child, I remembered some high cliffs on Aran Mór, where there were always strong winds. My fantasy was that Nancy and I walked to the top of the cliffs on a particularly windy day and when Nancy was peering over the edge, I pushed her over and said later a gust of wind had done it.

In my defence I should say that after 1959, when I received the correct medication for my condition, I was as incapable of physical violence as I had been before my illness. Also, I was totally dependent on the goodwill of others and lacking in any ability to assert myself, because my true self no longer existed and, for lack of it, I had forgotten the meaning to my life. This day-dream about Nancy was the final instance of my entertaining such violent thoughts, as medication had the effect of putting me in an entirely passive state, in which my only thoughts were purely intellectual or academic.

My parents were soon to realise that, for someone as severely schizophrenic as myself to have a loyal and accomplished wife such as Nancy must be very rare, and they thought that I should be content with having the sort of life which for most people like myself would have been unthinkable.

During the Easter holidays in 1966 Nancy sold the goodwill of our extremely comfortable council house to a family from across the Bullring so that we could all be together again. We put our furniture and possessions into a removal van, sat with the driver in his cab and moved to Rochdale, a half hour by bus from the college in Middleton.

Paul O'Rourke had told me that there were luxury flats available in tower blocks in Rochdale. I was so overwhelmed at the prospect of having Nancy and Seán with me, I had written to Nancy that our flat 'enjoyed a panorama of beauty'. On our arrival, Nancy pointed out wryly that the view consisted of the gasworks and a crumbling Victorian factory.

We soon found in any case that we were unable to afford the rent on the flat. At that point Nancy house-hunted and found a terraced house, at 176 Whitehall Street, so run down that even Third World immigrant families were refusing to buy it.

Nancy asked my parents if they would pay the mortgage on Whitehall Street and provide us with the deposit. They agreed. As Nancy said at the time, if my parents had not begun to help us from that point onwards, the alternative, unthinkable from their point of view, must have been that Nancy, Seán and I should live at Geragh.

As Nancy and I were living on my student's grant, Nancy hunted throughout Rochdale for a good builder we could afford. She found a seemingly reputable builder but, though he did the necessary work, he kept on buying cheap building materials, or asking for payment in advance and not turning up.

These were days of great hardship for Nancy, as not only did she feel it was necessary to work alongside the builder, but, as she always ensured that Seán and I had enough to eat, she often went hungry herself. Eventually we were able to move into Whitehall Street and I found she had again made a lovely home on a shoe-string budget.

During the summer holidays in 1966 I got work in a Bury cotton mill to supplement my grant. I thoroughly enjoyed performing my duties, which for once were within my scope. The other workers treated me like a visiting Eastern potentate as I was a student. The contrast between the way I had been treated as a busman in March and then as a Lancashire cotton mill worker was clear-cut and sweet – like a breath of early morning fresh spring air after leaving a stuffy house. Whereas the other March busmen had mostly tended to treat me as fit only for mockery, my fellow cotton mill workers treated me with respect and, what was most welcome to me, showed they liked me. Maybe the busmen saw me as no more than a help-less mental cripple and probably thought, at least in the early months of my time as a busman, that I would soon be sacked, whereas in Lancashire a teacher's certificate was regarded as being of some intellectual merit and I was treated accordingly.

I once asked one of my older workmates at the mill what he thought were the best years for us human beings. He smiled and after a little thought answered, 'Twenty-five to thirty-five. Them's the golden years'. I was thirty-two. One of my young workmates joked that, in the hypothetical event of my making a 'prestigious' success of my life, my doctors would by then be on the point of making arrangements for me to enter an old folks' home. At the end of the summer, when the autumn term was about to start, my three closest workmates, knowing I liked a pint of Guinness, took me to a pub above the valley and gave me a memorable send-off.

Over the next year I enjoyed the course-work but still found the teaching practices an ordeal. Telling myself I would make my fortune and prove myself worthy of Nancy and Seán, I finally ran away to London, in the middle of my final teaching practice in early June 1967. I can see today that I must have been very unhappy with my lot. As ever I expected too much from myself, perhaps because my ego still remembered my days of great promise at the King's Inns and I found it too difficult to accept that, as of 1957, my handicap made it impossible for those days ever to return. Nancy used to say to me later on that 'half a loaf is better than no bread', especially when many normal people were worse off than us, echoing what my mother used to say: that I was never satisfied.

When I reached London that morning I had a good supply of Stelazine but nowhere to stay, very little money and no plan of action. When the train arrived at the terminus, I read the newspapers at a stall. Before long, however, the newsvendor angrily asked me to move on. Evidently he saw me as a threat to his trade.

I first made for the hospital in Islington, where I knew I had been born. I saw a grim Victorian building, now North London University. Though I never felt suicidal, I needed to dispel my dark thoughts of inadequacy and loss and I wished to look at the place where, as far as I was concerned, my life had started to go wrong. Years later, after my parents had died, I learned the reason why I was the only one of my parents' children born outside Dublin. It seems that when my mother found out she was pregnant she did not tell my father. He was very sought after by women and as she did not wish him to feel pressurised into marrying her, she went to London, where she had spent most of her childhood, to have me.

She took me to Dublin when I was a few months old and, soon after, she was pushing me along in a pram when my father came towards us. When he looked in the pram he was immediately struck by the uncanny physical resemblance between himself and me. My mother and he were married in Dublin a short while later, before my three brothers and my sister were born. Now, with the benefit of this recent discovery, I can guess that I was perhaps driven to the former hospital by some primeval homing instinct. In the event I left my birthplace unenlightened.

A psychiatrist told me once that for the schizophrenic everything connected with himself is of heightened significance. In my own case I would add that I also suffered from an obsessive idea of my own exclusive importance. In my mind the world revolved around me. This was a symptom that Nancy and her sister-in-law had already remarked on when the three of us shared 56 Eastwood Avenue and it perhaps explains my behaviour at this time. I had no notion that my disappearance would appear incomprehensible to others, that anyone would be worried about me or that a search for me had been instigated.

I wandered to different areas throughout London. When evening came I was somewhere in South London and I made enquiries about a Salvation Army hostel. I was directed to what turned out to be a social services' hostel. After a night's sleep I was seen, along with others, by a psychiatrist. We were asked to go into a cubicle at the end of a long room. My psychiatrist was young and had a pleasant expression; he reminded me of Naunton Wayne, who partnered Basil Radford in films of the 1940s.

I told the psychiatrist I had run away from my final teaching practice at a Manchester college and added that I thought I had panicked. He must have agreed and thought no more about it, because I found myself free to leave.

Again I wandered aimlessly all over the city. Eventually I rang Geragh and spoke to my father. This conversation took place when I was at the Elephant and Castle tube station. My father asked for the number of the telephone and told me to wait. A little later Paul rang. Apparently it had been thought that I would be in London and Paul had volunteered to go down by train to look for me, while Nancy was comforted by his girlfriend.

Paul came by tube to the station and said he had arranged for us to visit the palace of the local Catholic bishop. We were given refreshments there before returning by train to Manchester.

My abandonment of Nancy and our child had made her distraught and she began to have doubts about our future, but it was two more years before total disillusionment with our relationship slowly overwhelmed her. She used to say then that I was my own worst enemy.

After Paul had brought me back from London in June 1967 my

mother came to stay in a Rochdale hotel to be near us for a couple of days. On her second evening she entertained Paul, Anne, Nancy and myself to dinner at her hotel. A priest attached to De La Salle, who was one of the two Catholic Canons of Divinity in England and Wales, also came to see me. I believe the Christian Brothers wished to check again that I was spiritually and morally fit to teach.

When I eventually did my final teaching practice in late June 1967 with some juniors I found it very demanding indeed, but the Christian Brothers were so determined that I get my Teacher's Certificate that, though again my performance was a borderline one, the examiner present from the Christian Brothers advised the lay examiner that I should be allowed to pass.

I look back with fondness to my days at De La Salle College and with extreme gratitude to the Christian Brothers; they had faith in me and I am sure they gave me the benefit of the doubt, on the principle that it is wrong to tar all people like myself with the same brush.

I passed both my French and English Final exams also, but with no great merit in either. Brother Vincent told me I had done disappointing exams in French. However, I was awarded the second highest grade with a Commendation for my Divinity thesis. It was about the time of Pope John XXIII and his championing of the cause of ecumenism. The local Bishop personally presented each of us with our certificates at the College.

6. In and out of school

I had been going for interviews for teaching jobs for some months while I was a teacher trainee. Some of the schools I applied to were boarding-schools in the private sector. I sent applications for posts all over England, but in July 1967 we decided to move back to March. We stayed temporarily with my parents-in-law at Peas Hill Road while I continued to apply for work. We used the same removal firm and travelled in the cab as before. Duly installed in Peas Hill Road again, I got another interview. This was to teach French and a little Remedial English to twelve- and thirteen-year-old boys and girls at the Richard C. Thomas County Secondary School in Bloxwich, Walsall.

In August 1967 I arrived for my interview at the Council Offices in Walsall. The interviewers were an official from the Council Education Department and the Head Teacher, a Mr Horace Lambe. Mr Lambe had a well-manicured moustache and thinning short dark hair parted in the middle, on which he appeared to use a liberal amount of hair oil and also, I suspected, Grecian 2000. He was a born teacher, living only for the welfare of his children. Maybe his instinct told him his teenagers would like me. Also, he may have found my academic track record impressive, as the Christian Brothers did. I saw him nod to the Council official and found I had the job. I was elated, especially when I heard I would be paid £1,000 a year. Even with all the available overtime my income as a bus conductor had never exceeded £500 a year. I was aware, though, that for my first school year I would be on probation.

I found accommodation with some younger teachers from other schools in a rural area of Great Barr. The couple I stayed with were constantly arguing in front of their two teenage children. I did a lot of reading and a Scottish teacher there lent me a copy of Robert Burns's poetry, which I much enjoyed. I occupied the evenings by doing a translation of Jean Anouilh's *L'Invitation au château*.

I spoke to my brother Brian at Geragh many times by phone during the autumn term. Perhaps the strain was telling on me as he kept urging me to keep a sense of perspective and, allowing for the basic requirements, to try and take my work in Walsall less seriously.

After Christmas my landlady asked me to find alternative accommodation. I suspect the reason was that she found my illness was of an unacceptable nature and severity, as others had before.

My new accommodation was in Bloxwich, much nearer the school, and was with an archetypal landlady called Aggie Potter. Diminutive, sparely built and unsmiling, she always wore a shapeless black dress and curlers and held the butt of a cigarette between her lips. It was down-at-heel accommodation. In the evenings the communal gas fire was kept on 'miser rate' and the guests were often given bread and dripping for supper.

As my cheerless room had no wardrobe, I was obliged to hang my clothes from a curtain rail. There were soup stains on one of my suits, the result of a meal with my aunts May and Hilda at their home near Geragh. For some reason Aggie Potter went into my room when I was out, saw the suit in question and became convinced that they were blood stains. Apparently at the time someone was driving around Walsall, picking up young girls and sexually assaulting and murdering them. Mrs Potter believed I was the man in question and, without telling me, took the suit to the local police station. After the suit had been forensically examined, I was allowed to collect it. For a time I was numb with shock and disbelief and then overcome with despair that, despite my conscientious efforts to lead a worthwhile life, it had been thought I might be capable of such a crime. Reassuringly, my mother pointed out to me that, apart from the fact I had never had homicidal tendencies, I did not drive anyway. This saved me from complete demoralisation.

Aggie Potter asked me to leave a few days later. Perhaps she remained unconvinced by the police evidence. Maybe Mrs Potter, like my Great Barr landlady, should have used her common sense rather than allowing my unconventional manner to convince her of my guilt. It is unfortunate for people like myself that the public view of my illness is shot through with misconceptions. Mrs Potter might better have understood my problems had she seen that I lived in a constant and uncompromising world of fanciful dreams, which left me slow to react to anything outside myself. Sadly, she and most others saw me, because of my St Vitus' Dance-like movements, as a coiled spring that at any moment might be released with great force.

For the next four to six weeks I stayed at a Salvation Army hostel in Walsall and commuted by tram to the school in Bloxwich. I then found accommodation in Chasetown with an Indian undergraduate studying Architecture at Aston University, called Mr Saini—I never knew his first name—and we were joined after a few weeks by his sister. The house was a modest semi on an estate and, though not as comfortable as Great Barr, was a distinct improvement on Aggie Potter's quarters.

I commuted regularly by bus and a fellow passenger called Brian Jones befriended me. It turned out he also was a Catholic and he took me with him to private Mass several times in the houses of his friends. He was a keen amateur astronomer and enjoyed showing me the sky at night through the telescope in his back garden. His wife, a sweet woman, usually stayed at home as she was expecting their first child.

On one occasion, Mr Saini entertained some fellow Hindus, Brian, two or three fellow Catholics and myself, and we discussed the relative merits of Hinduism and Christianity. Regrettably, the debate soon degenerated into a shouting match, with no one listening to anyone else. Afterwards Mr Saini said to me, in a way which I thought was unnecessarily defensive, 'We're not all duffers, you know.'

The Head of the French Department at the Richard C. Thomas School was a Mrs Battersby. She supplied me with the children's textbooks and stationery, which I soon found to my disappointment were in short supply. She did not rule me with a heavy hand. Mr Lambe asked me at the start to keep written records of my preparations for lessons and of the daily class progress. This I did scrupulously to the day I left. I never found out what Walsall Education Authority made of them, but should have liked to do so.

The school was in a deprived inner city area. Many of the boys and girls were ill-clad and ill-shod and some came from broken homes. I sensed early on the children liked me. From the start I very much wanted to teach some French to as many as I could. Despite any problems they may have had at home, those in my class and those I encountered throughout the school were refreshingly cheerful and, though full of the fun-loving joys of youth, to a child treated me with natural courtesy. However, by the very nature and severity of my illness, I was always going to have problems with classroom discipline. As an authorised teacher, I was obliged to take a firm stand, but I felt that the teachers and the children understood I was clearly a gentle person.

From the outset I had difficulty controlling classes and this got progressively worse. One day in the staff room Mr Groves, the Deputy Head, told me, probably correctly, that he did not think I was the right type for a teacher and Mr Lambe said to me at one point in the second term, referring to my neck movements, 'There's no need for all this nervous tension, Mr Scott.'

Fortunately I got on well with the teenagers. I got the impression that once they had tried and tested me, they approved of me, despite my practical incompetence as a teacher. I heard on the grapevine that among themselves they referred to me as 'Old Brassneck', but both inside and outside the classroom they addressed me as 'Sir' in a pleasant and respectful manner. Among the children in my class whom I remember were David Benson, Sylvia Barratt and Julie Hazeldine. When standing in for other teachers, I also taught David's twin sisters Carol and Beryl and 'the terror of the school', red-haired John Bates. I like to think that during this year, the most worthwhile of my life, I may have managed to teach a handful of children at least the rudiments of basic French.

Occasionally we had social events at the school and one evening before Christmas we had a school dance. The boys and girls were naturally rather awkward about dancing together. The highlight of the evening came towards the end when Mr and Mrs Lambe did a solo dance for the assembled company, a stately military two-step.

I was scrupulous about taking my medication while I was in Walsall. There was no Nancy nearby to take me to task so perhaps I had learned something from my De La Salle days about my need for it. It is true to say that the chemical causes of my particular disorder make medication vital; with this, it is possible for the patient to cope outside a hospital as long as there is support from family and friends. Scientists have not yet discovered a medicine which can completely cure the patient and today's treatment does little more than stabilise the sufferer, who remains mentally disturbed and in some ways unpredictable, but who is in most cases a threat to no one except himself.

I wish that other people could have understood that I posed no threat to them, however. One Sunday I arrived late for Mass in Walsall having travelled there by bus from Chasetown. (I went to Mass every Sunday during my year in Walsall.) As I was late, I walked briskly through the doorway and up the aisle until I found a seat. I suppose it is true that the movements of the severely ill schizophrenic are on the face of it cause for alarm, but I felt hurt when after Mass the celebrant mentioned my entrance into church, saying with a smile but with genuine conviction, 'I thought you were going to attack me!' I was bewildered because, as ever, I was only vaguely aware I had an alarming presence. Time and time again some misunderstanding person like the priest would react to me in a way that was antipathetic to my intentions and deeply distressed me as all I longed for was to be accepted as I had been in my youth. Also no priest had reacted to me like that before. In those days it was not uncommon for various equally misunderstanding people to infer from my appearance that I was an amoral and wicked person, and thus my morale was the more weakened by this episode. Up to that point I had seen any priest I met as being closer to God than my dearest relations and my belief in the sanctity of the priesthood was the more undermined as he said this within the hearing of several other members of the congregation. After this episode I began to see that not every priest is worthy of being known as a spiritual leader of men.

On another disturbing occasion, I was travelling on the top deck of a bus in the area. Just behind me on the other side of the aisle were sitting a shabbily dressed young couple holding a toddler. Because in my De La Salle days I had found children liked me, I kept turning round in my seat to study the small child. As I saw it, I was assessing the child's potential. I may have been thinking of the Jesuit Fathers' saying that if a child in its formative years, or up to about the age of seven when it reaches the age of reason, is put into their hands, they will be able to develop that child's full potential in a way that will last for life.

After about five minutes, the child's father looked at me darkly and said, in a loud voice, that if I did not stop looking at the child he would come over and hit me. I was thoroughly shocked and alarmed and looked fixedly out of the window for the rest of my journey.

When I told my story in the staff room one of the senior teachers said that if the young man on the bus had struck me a blow he would have 'ended up behind bars'. I found his words reassuring, but the experience badly affected my confidence. At that stage I believed I could cope with teaching, but I think now that I had by then lost some of my former insight into myself. Perhaps Dr Clark, though unquestionably well-meaning, had tried to get me to aim too high for the nature of my very severe limitations. Nevertheless, it means a great deal to me to have been a professional teacher for an academic year and I am grateful to have been given the opportunity.

At the end of the year I resigned from my job as Nancy and I wanted to be together, but could not afford house prices in Walsall.

When I was about to leave for March, I heard that Walsall Council had allocated us a council flat. However, Mr Lambe refused to allow me to withdraw my resignation saying that, as the children had come to know me, they would give me even more impossible discipline problems were I to carry on for the next year. For some reason, until he mentioned it the prospect of another year or more of similar tension and strain had never once struck me as being too much for me.

Happily, I parted from the Richard C. Thomas County Secondary School on good terms with Mr Lambe, the other teachers and the children; though it was a tough school and I had my difficulties, I nevertheless felt privileged to have spent a year as a teacher there.

With my mother and my father, 1934.

Geragh from across Scotsman's Bay, with the James Joyce Martello Tower on the right.

*My mother, Ciarín, myself, Michael, Brian and Niall
outside Geragh.*

Outside the Institut Montana in the snow, 1950.

With Ciarín in Sneem, Co. Kerry, 1953.

My mother and Aunt Betty, Italy, early 1950s.

In O'Connell Street, in the late 1950s—the strain of my illness beginning to show.

Niall and Mary's wedding, in Co. Kerry, 1964.
Back row: *John Nixon, Fr Dónal O'Sullivan, Bobby Guirey, Robin Walker, Dorothy Walker, Patrick Scott (no relation), Peg Ryan, Nan Ryan.*
Intermediate row: *Aunt May, Aunt Hilda.*
Middle row: *Brian, Ciarín, my father, my mother, Rita Ryan, Louis Ryan, Nora Guirey.*
Front row: *Michael, Geraldine Ryan, Louise Ryan, Niall, Mary, myself.*

With Seán, mid-1960s.

*With Nancy and Seán outside Geragh,
mid-1960s.*

My father with the Queen, 1975.

My father's 80th birthday party, 1985. Back row, left to right: Niall, Ciarín, Brian. Front row, left to right: Michael, my father and myself.

With Nancy and Seán, 1985.

Holding up a portrait of myself, drawn by Seán, 1986.

At Aunt May's 80th birthday party, early 1990s.

Reading outside the bungalow by the River Nene, September 1999.

7. Troubled about Nancy

In the autumn of 1967, shortly after I left March to take up my short-lived teaching career, Nancy and Seán moved to Ramsey, near March, in what was then Huntingdonshire. Nancy rented a first-floor flat from her sister Louie at 8 Bury Road. Louie herself lived in a prefabricated bungalow a few yards up the drive. From then on Nancy and Louie became as close to one another as they had been when they were children.

I returned home to Nancy and Seán in Bury Road in July 1968 and there I received notification from the Department of Education and Science that because of my discipline problems my probationary period was to be extended for another six months. Mr Lambe had advised me to get a job in a small country junior school.

I went to see Dr Clark at his out-patients' clinic at Benet Place in Cambridge. Perhaps because he was pleased I had held down a teaching job for a year, he took me into Fulbourn Hospital and took me off the Stelazine medication. He knew I hated being dependent on medication and may have seen this gesture as a psychological motivation which would make me determined to get through the remainder of my probation successfully.

In 1968, during my Walsall year, I had written to Leeds University with a view to reading for an Honours Degree in French Language and Literature. A little later I had taken a day off from teaching and travelled to the University to do some written tests. In late

1968 I rang the French Department at Leeds University from the hospital and they confirmed they would give me a place to start in October 1969 if I could get a grant. Studying French as a 'mature student' of thirty-six at Leeds University would mean doing a three-year instead of the usual four-year course, as one was exempted from spending a year in France. With hope springing eternal, I enjoyed my remaining weeks in hospital more than usual.

Dr Clark discharged me just before Christmas, and I went back to Ramsey. At this time Nancy was negotiating for us to buy a house on the Cam in Cambridge and had the promise of my father's backing. She thought that I might wish to change from Leeds University to Cambridge University. Eventually the Cambridge house, which apparently was an old house full of character and charm, was found to have subsidence, so I did not get the chance to sit the Cambridge University entrance examination.

It proved to be fortunate that we had moved from March to Ramsey, as Ramsey was then under a separate Education Authority, called Huntingdon and Peterborough. Like most Education Authorities, Cambridgeshire does not normally award a second student grant. It turned out, however, that the Huntingdon and Peterborough Education Authority was prepared to award me a university grant so that I would be qualified to teach to 'A' level.

Sadly for my plans, however, by early March Nancy began to see signs of a relapse in me once the Stelazine had entirely left my system. Our family doctor put me on Valium. Two days later, after Nancy and I had made love the previous night, I shook her hand at the front door and ran away by bus, train and ferry to Geragh. Within a few hours of my arrival, I was in a Dublin state mental hospital called St Brendan's.

I was put into a Victorian building for long-stay male patients of all ages, but mainly elderly. The wallpaper was peeling from the walls, the carpets were threadbare, the ceiling was stained brown from nicotine and in places there was human waste on the floor. After lights-out, a few of the particularly disturbed patients prowled in and out of the dormitory and the latrines all night. I was afraid to let myself fall asleep for even two or three hours lest my throat be slit by a misappropriated razor. When I was studying English as part of my Leeds University course over a year later, I was able to reflect that Miss Havisham's quarters in *Great Expectations* compared very favourably with my St Brendan's long-stay ward. Conditions there were infinitely worse than those at the fee-paying St Patrick's Hospital. After a couple of days my mother visited me. As she and I were talking, a young patient with a fixed stare asked her for a cigarette, which she gave him. Before leaving, she looked at me lovingly and whispered 'Trust me!' Later that day, I was transferred from the Victorian building to a new building for mixed short-stay patients.

Throughout these weeks my one thought was that I wanted to leave Nancy. Though I knew she was well-meaning, since my time at De La Salle I had instinctively felt that not only was she the wrong person to bring out the best in me, but that in some ways she was pulling me down. As I saw it, I was faced with Hobson's choice. I could either return to Nancy and never fulfil myself, or remain for life in this grim institution. From my disorientated and discontented point of view, my need for her was only as my minder and sexual partner. I kept coming back to the idea that I needed someone like Nancy who was also a cultural soul mate. Whether or not the need I felt was rational, it existed totally unbeknown to my conscious self, and persisted throughout our marriage and for some years beyond. At least part of the trouble was my inability to accept marital responsibilities. Eventually sex proved not to be enough for either of us.

After a few more days without any Stelazine in my system, my health deteriorated even further. I was at the stage where I had no control at all over my hyper-active and distressed mind, but even while I was at this deplorably low ebb, I did not feel any urge to behave violently, as I had built up a solid repertoire of stabilised experiences over the previous ten years thanks to the Stelazine and my stable domestic circumstances. Dr Gerry O'Gorman, my psychiatrist, with whom as a fellow-student I had played on the sports fields of UCD, contacted Dr Clark, who advised him to put me on injections of a new medication called Moditen. Within two or three days I was my old self again. Persuaded by my parents, I saw that I had no choice but to go back to Nancy. At first Nancy refused to have me, saying she would take Laurence and Seán and start a new life in Australia, but she eventually relented.

Nancy's own health suffered greatly during the eighteen weeks that I was in St Brendan's. Our relationship was never to be quite the same again. She had virtually lost her conviction that, with Seán doing well at school and herself as the home-builder looking after me, I had a worthwhile future. I had been in St Brendan's for nearly four months when Nancy wrote in our engagement diary that I had written to her saying I wished I could want to return to her but that, in fact, I did not. She added 'God help him and me for the future'.

My parents had always had doubts about whether Nancy was the right person for me, but fortunately for me, and perhaps also for Nancy, they were sure by that time that I should have no hope of coping outside a hospital without her. This was encouraging, but her own rock-like faith in what I could achieve with herself at my side had begun to be shaken to its foundations. I returned home to Ramsey in July, unaware that my many weeks away were to have a devastating effect on Nancy's emotional and physical health.

8. My degree

Nancy and I got the train to Leeds in September. A friend of my father's, Nigel Fitzgerald, who was the Chairman of Wimpey, had put his head man in the Yorkshire area, Harry Bamford, at Nancy's and my disposal. Mr Bamford met us at the station and took us to a comfortable boarding-house he knew of. It was run by a Scotsman, Harry Michael, and his wife, Anne, who could not have been more generous and welcoming. We spent about two weeks with them and each day Mr Bamford drove us over Leeds looking at property. As in Rochdale, my father intended to pay the deposit and the mortgage when we found a house.

One evening that month Nancy had a sudden and acute attack of asthma and had to take to her bed. We had been about to go out with Mr Bamford to do some house hunting, when she found she had great difficulty in breathing. The attack was the first she had suffered from. A chest consultant, Dr Gordon Edwards, diagnosed chronic bronchial asthma and put her on cortisone tablets and inhalers.

While Nancy and I were busy looking for a house, my father paid a flying visit to Leeds. While there he lavishly entertained Nancy and myself at some of the best restaurants, together with Mr Bamford, a colleague of his and an estate agent called Tom Thwaites. We eventually chose a three-bedroom semi, with an attractive garden, off Scott Hall Road at the end of a cul-de-sac. Nancy and I went back briefly to our Ramsey flat and in early October I returned on my own to Leeds. Again Mr Bamford met me at the station. He took me to some student accommodation where they had a room for me. The Hostel of the Resurrection was administered by a High Anglican community of clergymen for university students. At one of the social functions I saw Bishop Trevor Huddleston, the celebrated anti-apartheid campaigner from South Africa, at close quarters.

At the Hostel of the Resurrection I continued my uninterrupted and lifelong practice of going regularly to Mass and taking the Sacraments. Back in the days when I was a bus conductor, I had gone into the Catholic church in March once when it was empty. I knelt at the back and in a moment of intense anguish and despair over my psychiatric sufferings cried out at the top of my voice 'God help me!' However, when I went back to university and started to use my mind again in the way that I had been trained to do, I found life slightly easier to cope with and my sufferings were correspondingly reduced. Once Nancy and I moved into Stainbeck Walk during the Christmas vacation in 1969 I stopped practising my religion altogether. With the benefit of hindsight, I have absolutely no regrets about having been a lapsed Christian since then. Some of my worst moments of despair came when I was a law student and I tried abortively to practise the religion of my forefathers at the parish church of St Joseph's near Geragh. Not only did it take me until a few years ago to realise that I was never going to benefit from one of God's rare miracles, but also to see that it matters less that I practise my religion formally, inevitably failing to have true faith because of the very nature of schizophrenia, than that I keep on taking my medication and live a decent life. If religion is about someone turning towards his or her Maker with a childlike heart, it is beyond the severe schizophrenic, even with today's improved medication. Modern medication is effective, notwithstanding one view that it is 'crude and indiscriminate'. Certainly I personally would have no chance of surviving without it. Unfortunately, however, the wonder drug which might allow people like myself to adopt and benefit from formal religious practice, is unlikely to be discovered for several more generations. I believe that it is because my expectations from religion were too high that I invariably felt let down. Maybe less severely ill schizophrenics would get more than I did from going to church regularly.

My apparent religious indifference might be a little less difficult to understand if one remembers that one of the definitions of schizophrenia is that the seat of the intellect is separated from the seat of the emotions. This was explained to me by a Church of England minister while we were walking through the grounds of Fulbourn Hospital, shortly after my arrival from Dublin in the early autumn of 1958. His view was eventually substantiated by my psychiatrist of many years later, Dr Anthony Flood. I understood then why I tended to become overcome by the emotion around me when I was with others at Mass and, being unable to cope, to make animal sounds of distress, which alarmed those nearest to me.

When I started to read for my degree, it took a year to get the wheels of my mind working at the right rate. For the required two subsidiary subjects in the first year I chose English Language and Literature, and Greek Civilization. Greek Civilization was an unwise choice and I failed the examination in May 1970. When I passed the resit in the September, my delighted mother said to me on the telephone, 'A million, million congratulations!' She was particularly glad about this as she felt that I had at last a realistic hope of eventually passing my degree. I was able to drop Greek Civilization after my first year but continued with English, though this was not the least difficult subsidiary subject I might have chosen either. I barely passed the examinations at the end of each of my three years.

I felt more at home with French and was pleased to be taking it as my main subject. Professor Hope taught us the Language element of the course. This included Phonetics, Semantics and Linguistics, dealing with the pronunciation, meaning and use of French words and phrases. Professor Philip Thody was responsible for teaching us French Literature, which I particularly enjoyed.

After one of the French lectures early in my first term the lecturer came and chatted to various students. He eventually came over to me and told me, to my surprise, that he did not intend to single me out to answer questions because he could see I was 'one of the weaker brethren'. With hindsight I can see that his words were well-intended, but up to then I had been tending to see myself as the gifted student I was in 1955, thus lulling myself into a false sense of security. This conversation helped me realise that the teaching staff knew that I would be able to graduate only provided I managed to push myself well beyond the limits of my handicap. Fortunately for me, one of Ciarín's closest friends was in charge of the French Departmental Library and her husband was one of our lecturers. With their unfailing moral support Susan and Jim Dolamore greatly helped to make my path to graduation possible. By dint of determination and perseverance, I managed to stretch my powers of concentration far beyond what I had achieved in my training college days and I started the second year with a more than even chance of getting my degree.

There was one particular fellow-student at Leeds University whom I remember well. This was Swiss-born Françoise Logan, who was married to a Leeds surgeon. Françoise was a highly attractive mother of young children. She was a brunette like my mother and when she had been to the hairdresser and gave the world one of her radiant smiles, I found my legs becoming like jelly. I have always tended to react to beautiful women like a rather irresponsible adolescent. Happily for all concerned, our relationship did not develop beyond my schoolboy fantasies.

Françoise occasionally gave me a lift as far as my connecting bus and one day when lectures were over I persuaded her to drive me all the way home to meet my wife. Nancy had not met Françoise before and looked a bit taken aback. She showed her over the house, while I remained downstairs in my vegetative state. At one point I overheard her say to Françoise that without her I would not be able to survive.

Professor Thody had advised me that the best preparatory school in Leeds to send Seán to was called Moorlands. My parents stepped in and paid the fees. (Seán was a good pupil and benefited from his four years at Moorlands well enough to be awarded a scholarship to the prestigious Leeds Grammar School in 1974 when he was thirteen. He had a year at the school before we moved back to March.)

At about this time Nancy got a job in a nearby supermarket called Grandways. Her intention was to supplement my university grant which, though relatively generous, was not sufficient for our needs. In addition to paying Seán's school fees, my parents paid our mortgage, but Nancy paid our other bills, including the telephone bill on which I tended to make frequent long-distance calls to my mother. On one occasion, I asked my mother if we could have more financial help. She pointed out that she and my father simply could not afford to do anything more than they were already doing and also that Nancy, Seán and I were living better than most of our friends and relations as it was.

After her first bronchial asthma attack in September 1969, Nancy suffered many repeat attacks. Often when I was waiting for my bus to the University I could see Nancy at the stop on the far side of the road fighting for breath. Between Christmas 1969 and August 1975, when we returned to March, she was sent two or three times to a Leeds chest hospital, called Killingbeck Hospital.

I have felt recently that this illness was caused partly by the stress of her disillusionment with me and partly by her own nervous state. In 1959 she had been discharged from Fulbourn Hospital but her nervous condition was to return in 1969 and last until the day she died, deteriorating increasingly from 1975 to 1984 when a Harley Street psychiatrist, Dr Flood, diagnosed very severe clinical neurosis. Now that my own illness has eased a little I can look back at the dogged determination and courage Nancy displayed in facing up to her predicament with far more compassion and understanding than I could before.

Early in 1970 Nancy and I visited a woollen mill at Pudsey near Leeds to buy some material. The mill was closed, so we knocked at the door of an isolated house nearby to ask when it would reopen. A man came to the door, gave us the information we sought and invited us in. He offered us tea and said his name was Tom Grayson and that he lived there alone.

Mr Grayson took a great interest in Nancy and visited Stainbeck Walk several times. On one occasion he asked me somewhat archly, 'Is Nancy a good wife to you?', leading me to wonder if there was anything between them. However, Nancy had said to me two or three times in the course of our life together that if she were ever to be unfaithful to me, even once, she would feel obliged to leave me for the new man. As there was no suggestion that this was a possibility and because throughout the twenty-nine-and-a-half years we knew one another she displayed a conscience unique for its strength, I doubt if she had a relationship other than a platonic one with Mr Grayson.

In August 1970 I took nine-year-old Seán and three suitcases by ferry and train from Leeds to Bordeaux. We were met at the Gare St Jean in Bordeaux by my brother Michael, a lecturer at Bordeaux University, and were entertained by Michael and his Bordeaux-born wife Colette for two weeks at Michael's lakeside chalet, at the nearby holiday resort of Biscarosse. As it was August, all of France was on holiday. In the cool of the evenings Michael's father-in-law, Roger Hypoustèguy, who in addition to being a doctor was an excellent cook, would carry delicious samples of his expertise in the local cuisine over from his nearby chalet to ours. During the day the temperatures were considerably hotter than anything Seán and I had experienced and Seán developed severe sunburn. This might easily have become sunstroke, as Nancy said to me when she saw Seán's back, but luckily he recovered quickly.

When returning home Seán and I again changed trains in Paris and London. At one point the train from the Gare du Nord to Boulogne stopped for no apparent reason. Then two detectives from the Sûreté appeared at the door of our compartment. They were evidently searching the train for someone. One of the detectives asked me in French, 'Is the little one with you?' When I answered, 'Yes', they walked on. I was struck by the fact that the only person in the crowded compartment they spoke to was myself. By the time of this incident I had become more philosophical about the seemingly irreconcilable contrasts between my totally passive physical urges and the menace I appeared to be to those who did not know me well. I have wondered lately how much longer I will continue to give people the impression of being a threat when I am totally lacking in ill-intent and never have violent impulses towards anyone. Some of the people I meet regularly still react as if I am about to attack them, which I find extraordinary considering that many have known me for over forty years. Ironically, during the first five and a half years of my complaint, before I had any effective medication and on rare occasions was violent, my presence did not seem to give any cause for alarm.

Despite the incident on the French train, the most demanding part of our journey home was going by underground from Victoria to catch the Leeds train at Kings Cross. It was the rush hour, there was a heat wave, Seán was overtired and mischievous, we had to stand and the suitcases seemed heavier than usual. Up to that point I had considered that some of the journeys from Euston to Holyhead and Dún Laoghaire were made in the seventh circle of Purgatory. The underground journey that day made me think again.

Sometimes when Nancy had time off from work I took her and Louie, when she was staying with us, or one of Nancy's Grandways friends, to lunch in the Students' Union restaurant. I used to love seeing myself as being about to graduate and drinking in the ambience with Nancy at my side. I particularly enjoyed these lunches as I felt that for a refreshing change Nancy was benefiting from my own reflected glory rather than my father's.

Nancy was very attached to her father and it was distressing for her when he died in his sleep during an attack of bronchitis at the end of June 1971, while I was in France. Though as a mature student I was exempted from spending a year in France I still, like the younger students, had to spend ten weeks there in the summer of 1971 at the end of my second year. I actually spent nine weeks there, telling myself I wanted to rejoin Nancy a little sooner. In fact in some ways I dreaded returning to her, but again there was no alternative.

I went again to Bordeaux but this time I stayed with Roger Hypoustèguy and his wife, Odette, who was a teacher in a *lycée*, or grammar school. Their son, Daniel, his wife, Marie-Claude, and their five-year-old son also lived at the house. The Hypoustèguys spoke no English, so my few weeks there helped me with my language work. The whole family was very kind to me and made me feel very much at home. Daniel, who was a medical student, gave me my Moditen injections. On one occasion when I was having an injection I said to him 'I do miss my wife'. He replied 'That's normal', but I felt in those days I was at fault for not enjoying Nancy's company as much as I should have liked and needed to.

I attended daily lectures at the university. During the centenary of the Paris Commune, the students re-enacted the events on the campus. The celebrations were well attended. I remember thinking that, though France is as chauvinistic as any other country, in her case the universal national attribute has some uniquely redeeming qualities.

At one of the university lectures, the lecturer asked the class what was the meaning of the word 'horrere'. As I had done quite well in Latin at the age of sixteen when I had taken part of my university entrance examinations, and as no one else put up their hand, I raised mine. I offered the meaning that the word applies to dogs only; and that it applies when the hairs on the back of a dog's neck stand up in excitement, fear or anger. The lecturer appeared surprised that someone like myself should know the answer and complimented me on being a Latinist.

Sometimes one of the lecturers drove me from the university to a point where our routes diverged. After I had been dropped off on one such occasion, I was walking the mile to catch my bus to the Rue Joseph Brunet. Because of my disturbed mind, the sound of my footsteps is distinctive and tends to alarm anyone who does not know me. There was a young woman walking on the footpath ahead of me. She repeatedly looked over her shoulder at me in an apprehensive way. We seemed to be going in the same direction for several streets. Eventually the young woman stopped an approaching stranger, threw herself into his arms, pointed at me, told the stranger I was clearly about to attack her and asked for his protection. By this point she was hysterical. As I passed by them I heard the stranger, a middle-aged man, calming her down and assuring her that I was doing no more than going about my own business. Robert Burns thinks our lives might change if we could 'see oursels as others see us'. Would we be enlightened, edified, motivated to surpass ourselves, or simply disabused of our preconceptions?

Towards the end of my stay with the Hypoustèguys, Roger, Odette and I drove to St Émilion in the Dordogne, where I was giving them lunch. We had an excellent meal, washed down by a bottle of St Émilion, in a charming old-fashioned restaurant on the first floor with snow-white linen tablecloths and napkins. Afterwards we walked up and down the steep hills of the town to see a medieval charnel house. This was a large natural cave below ground level, into which dead bodies were thrown from a narrow opening above. We walked on to a disused monastery which now sells wine; the Hypoustèguys bought some and I bought a bottle of sparkling wine for Nancy because I knew she liked a glass, as she used to put it, 'after the sun has gone over the yardarm'. I learned that the French for sparkling wine is '*vin mousseux*' and used this knowledge to impress her later.

On my return home I found Tom Grayson no longer came to the house.

I particularly remember a French tutorial early in 1972, the year of my finals, given by Dr Malcolm Smith, for about nine or ten students. At one point Dr Smith threw a question at us. He asked us for the name of the naval battle in 1571 in which the hold over the Mediterranean of the Turkish fleet was decisively crushed by the forces of the Holy League. I remembered having read about it somewhere and said, 'The Battle of Lepanto'; I added that Miguel de Cervantes fought aboard a Holy League ship. For a moment there was silence. Then an astonished Dr Smith said, 'How did you know that?' I felt proud of myself.

In the two weeks leading up to our first examination in May, I worked more intensively than ever. Long after Nancy had gone to bed, I was still working. After midnight I walked around our lawns digesting what I had read throughout the course and putting it in order in my mind. I felt quietly confident; I knew that in the last three years I had stretched my mind far beyond what it had been capable of a few years earlier and I also felt I had the full support of Professor Thody, Jim Dolamore and the other lecturers.

Another student in my year told me I had passed when I was out shopping with Nancy. Though he did not know my grade, he said no one had failed, and that everyone had got honours of one class or another. When I went to the University the next day I saw to my great satisfaction that I had passed with Third Class Honours. Throughout the intervening years since then I have strongly felt that my degree would not have been possible, given the extreme severity of my illness, without the faith and support of my mother and my own faith in my abilities which gave me the strength to fight my way through. I am the more grateful for it, as Dr Moore, the psychiatrist at St Patrick's, had said that I would never be able to concentrate sufficiently to study again as an undergraduate, and indeed that it would be inadvisable for me to try to do so.

My degree

After our return to March a few years later, I went to see Dr Clark at his out-patients clinic in Cambridge. When I told him about my degree and at his request gave him the details about the Third Class, he said in a pleased and surprised way, 'This is a major achievement, Tony!'

The University's Chancellor, the Duchess of Kent, always presented the degree certificates personally. Being acutely self-conscious about my illness, including my neck movements, which I felt made me stand out like a sore thumb, I knew that I could not face the ceremony and I chose to receive my certificate *in absentia*, by post.

9. The worst of times

The following months brought peace of mind and a quiet sense of well-being. For a time the relationship between Nancy and myself regained a little of its former magic. Again I found myself applying for teaching jobs, though mostly of an unsuitable sort.

The reason I was applying for posts in a secondary school was that Huntingdon and Peterborough Education Committee was expecting me to teach to 'A' level. For some obscure reason I assumed they meant it to be in a state school, which was a mistake. A small day or boarding preparatory school post, or even a minor public school post, might have been more suitable than the job I did get.

Maybe the prospect of trying to control a classroom of lively teenagers once more put a strain on me. I believe this was why an incident occurred just after Christmas 1972, as I popped around the corner to the shops across Scott Hall Road. The road is one of the busiest in Leeds and has a dual carriageway and islands in the centre. I found myself hopping on one leg across the road to the island in rush hour traffic. There I paused, before continuing to cross in the same way. One or two cars almost swerved off the road as their drivers stared in disbelief. Maybe they regretted the last drink over lunch. My behaviour did not strike me as odd, because I was concentrating on the prospect of again tackling something that in my heart of hearts I knew was beyond me. My behaviour at home was often equally bizarre, though I was unaware of it. Seán used to watch me with distressed and astonished eyes as I walked about backwards round the house. Nancy sensibly took no notice.

In January 1973 I turned up at my new school, Batley High School for Boys. I was thirty-nine. My salary in Batley was £1,750. For the short time I was there, one of the teachers drove another teacher and myself for the half-hour journey. When I went into the staff room before lessons began on the first day of term the Head Teacher, Mr Willie O'Neill, built up everyone's expectations by saying the school was honoured to have a recent Honours graduate as a new member of staff.

From my first lesson, my discipline problems were even worse than they had been in Walsall. Here also I was responsible for the younger teenagers. The only occasion on which the stress was bearable was when I was an invigilator during an examination.

After five or six weeks the Head and Deputy Head called me into their respective offices. Whether courageously or rashly, I strenuously protested to both men that my discipline problems were not too much for me. Both were firm and said I'd have to resign. As Mr O'Neill put it, 'It's time for us to part company, Mr Scott'. As Mr Lambe had done, Mr O'Neill advised me to try to get work in a small junior school. He also gave me the references I asked for.

Again Nancy became disenchanted with me.

I started to advertise my services as house cleaner and gardener. I worked in several houses in both capacities, though most of my customers did not keep me long. Everything about me, from my movements to how I spoke, told everyone clearly that I was mentally ill, very disturbed and a seemingly very unpredictable man in his early middle age.

Around 1974, Nancy was getting off the bus to cross the road for her day at Grandways. She was wearing her uniform underneath her overcoat. An official from the Department of Health and Social Security, who was on the top deck of the bus, recognised her. I was receiving dole money at the time. We were both summoned to our local DHSS office then and soon after our return to March I was called into my DHSS manager's office. The manager told me that because of Nancy's and my own undeclared earnings while I was drawing dole, I owed the Department nearly £400, which would be taken out of my estate when I died. Today I realise I was lucky I did not have to go to prison. Although I later heard that the manager's words were normal in such cases, I was distressed in my paranoid way for some time.

Two households employed me for the last two-and-a-half years before we returned to March in August 1975. Mayo Jackson, a dentist, and his wife employed me as a cleaner and gardener. Mr and Mrs Hofmann, a barrister and a lecturer, gave me work as a house-cleaner. At the end of my first day Mrs Hofmann told me she could not fault my work at all.

The Hofmanns had three young sons and their nanny was an attractive local girl, Lesley. After my first day I did not see much of Mrs Hofmann or her husband. Over the time I was there I established a close friendship with Lesley. She was sympathetic whenever I spoke of Nancy and encouraged me to keep soldiering on.

No one knew that, at least since my St Brendan's days in 1969, Nancy was on the long painful road of her severe clinical neurosis. Nancy's illness took a particularly unpleasant form in that it made her manic with anything or anyone she could not cope with, and especially myself. If she regretted her marriage to me from early 1969 onwards, she regretted it even more in February 1973 when I had to resign my post at Batley Grammar School and much more again when we returned to March two and a half years later. Nancy was then fifty-one. On more than one occasion, she was to say she had been 'born under Capricorn', which must be the reason why she did not know whether her first or her second marriage had made her the unhappier.

My greatest crime was I simply could not help my behaviour. Given this very severe limitation, I'm pleased to think I never broke the law or intentionally scandalised anyone or hurt anyone's feelings. Again given my limitations, I tried always to compensate for the unfavourable first impression I knew I made on people, though my efforts were often without success.

One evening in 1974 there was a sign of things to come. Nancy, Seán and I were sitting around the dining table having supper. During our conversation Nancy hinted that once we were in March she might divorce me. It is possible that she said this as her way of encouraging me to get a good job, perhaps a post in a small junior school in the March area, and again surpass myself by carrying out my six months' extended probation successfully. Seán, who was then thirteen, was extremely upset and wept bitterly. Because I could not bear to see Seán in such a state, I said quietly, though without knowing what I could do to avoid one, 'There will be no divorce'.

Nancy had decided that she wanted to return to March to be near her mother and her son Laurence, by then a young man, and for my own part I was happy to return there because it was the only small country town I knew well and where we would be free of the stresses of city life.

Sadly, in February 1975 Nancy's mother, Rosella, died. Rosella, known usually as Ros, had always been extremely gentle and kind to me and had never taken me to task for my many shortcomings. She had often tried to stop Nancy from nagging at me and I missed her quiet influence. We had already sold 5 Stainbeck Walk and my father had bought us a run-down detached property on the River Nene and near March town centre. Nancy had always wanted to live by the river. With extreme difficulty Nancy got planning permission for the improvements she wanted; my architect brother Niall did the design free of charge and my father paid all the building costs. We had thought for a while of moving to York; we had visited there several times and Nancy had fallen in love with it as a more attractive and quieter place than its giant neighbour, Leeds, but the point of no return for us had already been reached before Ros's death. I cannot help feeling that had we gone to York, the novelty of such a move might have prevented the end of our relationship coming so soon and being so abrupt and so total.

In August 1975 I took my leave of the Jacksons and Hofmanns. Lesley came into the front garden holding the youngest Hofmann child in her arms, and saw me off. A short while later, the same March removal firm as before placed its services at our disposal for the fifth occasion. Nancy and Seán went by train and I travelled with the same driver as before in the passenger seat and as before helped him to load and unload our furniture and personal possessions. We stayed at 2 Peas Hill Road with Laurence and his girlfriend, Christine Fovargue, for two years while our house was being rebuilt and, from the day we arrived, Nancy and I were constantly at odds with one another.

What mystifies me is the way in which, though Nancy had already shown signs of discontent with our marriage in Leeds, suddenly, within hours of our return to March, her neurosis became very acute and remained so almost until her death. She had never before, even after my hospitalisation in St Brendan's, been so uncompromising about having to live with a paranoid schizophrenic like me. I can only think that our return to the town she had been brought up in was the catalyst which brought about her final disillusionment with our relationship.

In the autumn of 1975 a Social Welfare official, a Mrs Desborough, visited Nancy and myself at Peas Hill at Nancy's request. I believe the reason for her visit was to see if there was a case for institutionalising me. Though Nancy was always aware I could do nothing about my inadequacies as a partner, by then she was unable to face the prospect of being endlessly pulled down in her emotions, to be left bitterly disappointed and heartbroken. I believe that towards the end of her life she came to realise that she had had the same effect on me. We had effectively been pulling one another down from the moment that I began to study again in 1965; though this did not become fully clear to Nancy until 1984 and it took me another six years, until after I had fully recovered from losing her, to understand how much our emotions had been in conflict.

In early December 1975 I was invited with the rest of my family by the Royal Institute of British Architects to their headquarters at Portland Place in London for the presentation of their Gold Medal to my father. It was the time of the nearby Balcombe Street siege by the IRA, so my father in his speech of acceptance said he hoped the award would unite Great Britain and Ireland even more. Though my father was a great patriot he was totally opposed to violence. He told us afterwards that he and my mother had met the Queen in an ante-room before the ceremony.

The following December Ciarín rang me to say that my mother had had an accident at home and had died. The shock was terrible. I was utterly devastated and could not be comforted. I cried out while Ciarín was on the phone as I had done when I howled in the worst moments of my illness feeling myself to be in my own death throes, as much in despair about my future without her as in my total grief for her loss. My mother had always been my most loyal supporter and I missed her dreadfully. I lost my lifelong and only unconditional friend and my closest link with childhood. She had been particularly devastated by my disease. Because of the affinity between us, she had a rare insight into my agonies and mental incapacity. I believe my mother suffered for my sufferings as had no one else and the strain on her undoubtedly blighted her life. Until her death, on 3 December 1976, I took her and her unconditional and devoted goodness to me for granted. It was only after her death that I had any idea at all of what she had meant to me.

The next nine years was the worst period of Nancy's and my married life. When the three of us were staying with Laurence while our wooden shack was being brick-skinned, extended and modernised, Nancy made it clear that she found 'carrying' me to be too much of a burden. I felt instinctively that given the right circumstances she would try to get me out of her life. I tried to do as much work as I could on the small garden at Peas Hill and in the house itself, though sadly much of my work was not up to scratch.

Once again, the builder working on our new property turned out to be less honest and competent than we had expected. He spent a lot of time fishing, while saying he was waiting for materials to arrive, and used cheap materials though my father had paid for good quality. When the house was finally ready in late 1977, Nancy spent a couple of years making good his poor workmanship with her own hands and at further expense. She also made a terraced garden and boat jetty from what was virtually a rubbish tip. Because my father could only afford to give us a certain amount of financial help, Nancy ensured I did as much work on the house and garden as I could. As her asthma and her neurosis became more acute, she became manic about this. Because of the way she tyrannised me, these two forms of work became a nightmare for me. Though she was right to expect me to contribute some work, I began to dread it. She would ask me to vacuum, clean and polish throughout the house daily and was punctilious to the point of getting me to clean the grouting between the tiles in the kitchen, bathrooms and porch, every day. After a while we also acquired two allotments, on which I did most of the work. I often came home with bleeding fingers after prolonged bouts of digging. Sometimes I accidentally broke household objects and on two or three occasions Nancy was reduced to pummelling me with her fists in sheer despair. Unfortunately I was totally unable to respond to her distress in anything other than a negative and passive way and it is only with hindsight that I can see she badly needed psychiatric help herself.

At some point in the late 1970s Nancy tried to get Invalidity Benefit for me. This would have eased the financial strain on us considerably. Unfortunately for the two of us I did not get this until early 1985, by which time I was assessed as requiring Severe Invalidity Benefit.

Among the many visitors to our new house was Nancy's sister Louie, a mild-mannered, gentle person who had a beneficial influence on Nancy and often helped me to cope with her. Louie had a boyfriend, an antique dealer called Jim Jackson, who was estranged from his wife. On one occasion we were all drinking tea around the dining-table at home and Nancy was getting distraught about my shortcomings. Jim, probably to frighten me into doing more on Nancy's and my own behalf than I was already trying to do, threatened to 'stick a knife in my stomach' if I did not work harder. His words had a traumatic and negative effect, merely feeding the paranoid element in my mind, without encouraging me to do better.

Once Nancy and I had made the house and garden as we wished them to be, I started applying for work in a local state junior school. When I went out to the Local Education Authority in Peterborough an official told me I would be given a post only provided the Head Teacher concerned gave me an unsalaried post for my first six months. He said that if at the end of that period I had passed my extended probation, the Authority would pay me a salary. It was a way of saying I was not wanted as a teacher. This I found out for certain when none of the several junior school Heads in the March area would take me on under those conditions. It was the end of my teaching career. I realise now the Deputy Head at Walsall was right; even with all the will in the world I would never have made a teacher.

Depressed by my failure to get a job and extremely unhappy at home, I became even more disturbed than usual and this led me to a course of behaviour which might have had dire consequences. I have received my medication by injection since 1969 and have the treatment regularly at March Health Centre, where a nurse injects me. In 1979, over a period of about three months, I was going down to the Health Centre and asking one of the three nurses for my Moditen up to twice a week. As the prescribed interval was once every ten days, this caused some alarm when it was discovered and a London doctor said I was lucky not to have had permanent brain damage. I have always found it hard to understand how the over-dosing went on for so long undetected.

Louie fell ill in 1981 and was found to have a cancerous brain tumour. She had a course of chemotherapy after which she came round to see us several times, but the next thing I knew was that she had been sent to Fulbourn Hospital, where she died that June. Nancy was distraught; she had lost a dear sister and her own last link with her childhood.

In 1983, Nancy was admitted to Peterborough District Hospital with an asthma attack. She was too breathless to talk and the ambulance-man had to lift her from her bed at home on to a stretcher before carrying her to the ambulance. I visited her several times during each of her stays in hospital. She did not lose her sense of humour at any time, which helped me to cope.

However, Nancy had begun to distance herself from me even more. When in 1983 I prolonged my planned two-week visit to Michael and Colette in Bordeaux to fourteen weeks, the reason was that I dreaded returning to Nancy because of her hysterical attitude towards me. At the time she appeared to be uncompromising and cruel.

Finally realising the brutal truth that we were incompatible, Nancy said to me, 'One of us is going to die and I'm determined it's not going to be me'. This shocked me as I had not consciously seen the situation like that. As ever throughout our life together, in spite of everything, and perhaps because of my spiritual and emotional needs, I was unable to accept things as they had become and was convinced we were still in love. Nancy's neurosis and my mental health became worse than ever. In 1983 when my father stayed with me for what was to be the last time, he said to me as we were saying our goodbyes: 'Nancy's mind is in a terrible state. Do everything she asks and be gentle with her. And for goodness' sake, don't argue with her.'

By July 1984 the strain of an impossible situation for us both proved too much for Nancy. At her request, I was admitted to Adrian Ward in Fulbourn Hospital on 27 July. One of the reasons for my admission to the ward, which was for short-stay mixed patients, was to change my 1969 Moditen to a sister drug, Modecate, which has no sedative side effects. In the event the change of drugs was effected successfully. Another reason was so that Nancy could have a break from looking after me. After a few days I realised that this particular stay in a mental hospital was allowing me more peace of mind than I would have thought was possible in such a place and I found I was popular with the other patients and with the staff. As Dr Clark had retired the previous year, however, the quality of medical care left a lot to be desired. A couple of the nurses showed some interest in my degree, but, under the circumstances, this seemed rather irrelevant to me. I was given kitchen duties; after meals I had to clean the containers the food arrived in from the hospital kitchens, and also the draining boards and two sinks. I took my chores seriously and each time spent an hour or more on them.

I was enjoying the company of other patients more than I ever had before and one friendship, established during my twelve weeks in hospital, is still going strong. Laurence's mother-in-law, Joy Fovargue, was admitted to Adrian Ward some weeks after myself, suffering from manic depression. After my discharge, Nancy, Joy, myself and mutual friends used to get together and our contact re-established itself when Nancy died. For years Joy and I visited each other regularly and I found that I valued Joy's company for the easy friendship it offered.

In early August, Nancy rang May and Hilda, and said she felt, despite her conscience about me, that she would have to leave me for Seán's and Laurence's sake and to save herself. Nancy also told me later that Hilda thanked her for giving me twenty-four good years under circumstances which had been more devastating than anyone could possibly have foreseen.

Nancy was now sixty and I had reached fifty the previous November. I later learned from my father that my illness should have begun to burn itself out any time from about autumn 1983. This at least was what back in 1958 Dr Carstairs of the Maudesley had felt would happen. In fact by 1984 I was still as withdrawn as ever. I now realise that if I had not wanted to start using my powers of concentration again, the relationship between Nancy and myself would not have been nearly as bad for either of us, but Nancy was attracted by the idea of seeing me successful in my chosen career and I was driven inexorably on towards self-fulfilment by the memory of my former capabilities. I also know that, given my extreme clinical helplessness and vulnerability, it is inconceivable that I could have survived as long as I have if Nancy had not been there.

I should point out that over these years I was in the care of various GPs. The impression I got from certain of them was that their training in psychiatric medicine had been inadequate and they were unwilling to make the effort to understand my case. I felt there was no rapport between us and I was little more than a number in their files. On a few occasions Ciarín and Niall crossed swords with doctors whom they felt were not up to the mark in their treatment of both Nancy and myself. Being treated with coldness and indifference did not help my morale, especially at times of crisis in my life. The unfortunate attitude of some of the March townspeople towards me had also undermined my already weakened self-esteem. Thankfully, as a rule I found psychiatrists, close friends and relatives far more sympathetic.

While I was in Fulbourn, I kept in contact by telephone with my father, Michael, Brian, Niall and Ciarín. Niall and Ciarín drove down from their London homes to visit me on a couple of occasions. At one point Niall said he thought I might have to remain in hospital for two years. From my perspective, this meant inevitable and early mental decay and death, and I was very alarmed. My father told me that if Nancy left me matters would be very serious for me.

Eventually Nancy arrived looking thin, pale and drawn. She told me that while she had been staying with Ciarín and her husband, Tim, in London she had had a total nervous breakdown which had been worse than the one she suffered in 1958. She was sustained by Ciarín and by Sheila Nethercott, Ciarín's daughter Cara's nanny. She could remember nothing of her fortnight there except, vaguely, Sheila's and Ciarín's kindness. It was at this time that Ciarín found her a great and compassionate psychiatrist in Dr Anthony Flood, who diagnosed her illness as the severe clinical neurosis I have mentioned. He prescribed tranquillisers which Nancy took until a couple of years before her death. Dr Flood told Nancy when he heard I was a patient there, that he felt that since Dr Clark's retirement Fulbourn had become 'the Bognor Regis' of British psychiatric hospitals. Fortunately for me, Dr Flood became my own psychiatrist when I came out.

Nancy and I sat in the dining room of the hospital during her visit. She told me that, while he was working in Ireland, Seán had got caught up in the Hare Krishna cult, and that she was approaching every appropriate organisation to try to free him; he was sending her strange letters and photographs of himself and other Hare Krishna followers, with shaven heads and saffron robes. Nancy was one whose faith was in her heart rather than in exterior religious observances, but she felt that Christianity was the only religion worthy of mankind. When she described the Hare Krishna cult as anti-Christian, I was overcome with grief and sobbed bitterly. I felt profound sadness for my only child's predicament, and for Nancy and myself.

Years before, my GP had prescribed Mogadon for my chronic insomnia. Throughout the late 1970s and early 1980s I was only able to sleep for one night in two, even with the Mogadon, and I used to sleep throughout the second day. Though the prescribed limit is two pills, I found myself taking more and more until, before admission to hospital this time, I was taking ten to twelve. When Nancy accepted me back home on 20 October, I was still dependent on them.

Withdrawn as I was into my shell, all I could do for Seán was to leave his release from the Hare Krishna people entirely in Nancy's hands, which I did in total trust, knowing that she would find a way. Though, pulled down emotionally by her own mental state and my illness, she found the situation increasingly difficult, she eventually succeeded in getting Seán to come home in December 1984. I was relieved and very glad to see him. However, Seán, who had always lived at home and had shared in the traumas of his parents' relationship, was profoundly disturbed by his recent experiences and began to take the same number of pills from my Mogadon bottle, as he could not sleep either.

This was the last straw. In January 1985 I asked my GP to wean me off Mogadon. He did and I never took sleeping-pills again. Neither did Seán. I do not know to this day how Nancy did it, but by the summer of 1985 she managed, with the help of Seán's new girlfriend, Rita Duddy, to wean Seán away from the cult and break its stranglehold on his mind for good.

I found that the three months in hospital had benefited me considerably. Other people seemed also to notice the improvement. The landlord of my local pub just could not believe I was my old self again.

However, from early 1986 my health began to deteriorate once more. Nancy and I had already tried to re-establish the marital relations we stopped after we left Leeds eleven years before, but I found I had become impotent in the interval and this compounded my problems.

In August 1986 Michael invited Nancy and myself to his home in Paillet, a small village about twenty miles south-east of Bordeaux, for a couple of weeks. When we were at Heathrow, Nancy was again as abrupt and cold as she had been up until my admission to hospital. In Paillet we slept in an old 'tower' attached to Michael's 18th-century farmhouse home. My self-respect had sunk to as low a level as ever it did. I began to sleep fully clothed. This was a habit I carried on till I had been a widower for some time.

At my request, Michael drove Nancy and me to Lourdes for a day. It was my first visit to a Marian Centre—a place where there have been apparitions of Our Lady—since I had been there with my parents in 1958, but this time the mystery was not sufficient to prevent Nancy and myself acting out a sequence from a relentless nightmare to find ourselves arguing in the uppermost of the three churches.

Between October 1987 and September 1989, Dr Flood reduced my Modecate dosage in gradual stages by forty per cent from its original strength. He established the new dosage as the irreducible minimum for me and it has since been maintained at this level. I know now the importance of having it and am careful never to miss an injection.

Nancy became physically very weak after Christmas 1987. We had been getting my Severe Invalidity Benefit since about March 1985, so we could afford to eat lunch out six days a week and I prepared something simple for our suppers and Sunday lunches. I also did the shopping, as I had been doing for four years, and collected her prescriptions for cortisone and inhalers and had them dispensed.

Before her nervous crisis in 1984 and subsequent declining physical health, she had had many friends, most of whom she entertained at home. She was known as a caring and conscientious person and had offered a shoulder to cry on to many people with varying personal problems. Now no one came to the house and all her former friends seemed to have vanished.

During her last weeks, once she realised she was losing her fight for life, she became resigned to her fate. We said the sort of things to one another that we used to say when we first met. These tender words meant even more to me when eventually I began to recover from the pain of losing her.

Laurence's first child was then about eighteen months old and Nancy delighted in being with her. On the day before she died, a Sunday, Nancy was expecting Laurence to collect her to take her to his house nearby to see the young child as he usually did at weekends. Throughout the afternoon she kept looking at the clock in our living room but he did not come. Heartbroken, he told us later that something to do with his business had cropped up at the last minute.

Nancy's last thoughts may well have been of the new human life in the family, whom she had so much wanted to see again, for what, as it turned out, would have been the last time.

As we sat at our dining table on the day before she died, Nancy told me that the previous evening she had felt an acute stabbing pain in her chest. She said this calmly and without a trace of fear, as if she knew what was soon going to happen. I was heartbroken, as I felt all was lost. I could see Nancy accepted that the end was near.

Nancy died aged sixty-four from an attack of breathlessness at about four o'clock on the morning of Monday, 9 May 1988. Seán's partner, Rita, found her in the living-room a short while later and alerted Seán and myself. She was wearing a torn night-dress she had intended to replace the next day. She was buried, at her own request, with her mother.

I was devastated, and would have been unable to begin to cope normally without the support of Seán, my brothers and sister and Dr Flood. Tragically for us both, what Nancy had thought when we married would be the uplifting effect she would have on my mental health had eventually turned out to be the opposite. After she died, I very nearly degenerated into the diseased vegetable I was before we first met. Having improved in 1959 with the help of the new medication and, equally vitally, the unconditional support of Nancy from being like a man who had lost the use of both legs and his right arm, I found after her death that it was as if I had lost the use of my left arm in addition.

10. Beginning to write

My father outlived my mother by a little more than twelve years. After she died and he had retired from his practice, he led a very full social life, some might say a little too full when he was advanced in years. Eventually he spent many months confined to bed before dying peacefully in his sleep on 24 January 1989 at the age of eighty-three. The local priest came to visit him every week during this time and I recall the ritual of Brian's dog, a Tibetan terrier, chasing him all the way from the front door to my father's bedroom on the third floor. It was always a race, with the priest showing a remarkable turn of speed. The slow passage of my father's last days gave him time to say goodbye to his many friends. I saw him for the last time when I stayed at Geragh with him and Brian for my birthday in November 1988. By this time he was almost totally bedridden, but on the day itself, to my surprise and delight, he dressed in his invariably impeccable style and came down to the drawing-room. We sat and talked for about twenty minutes before going into the dining-room for my birthday lunch.

For several years after Nancy's death, I found it extremely difficult to cope on my own. Few people in March offered me any support or sympathy and the nurses at the Health Centre were indifferent and cold towards me. I used to come home in such a state of tension that I found myself kicking the furniture and throwing things, once slamming a glass door so hard that it smashed, in my despair at how I was being treated. When I went to the pub, people used to make fun of me, mocking me and making faces at me; one man would put his hands to his ears, waggle his thumbs and stick his tongue out at me. I suffered at home too: two months after Nancy died her niece had given me a miniature Yorkshire terrier called Tiny. I looked after him very irregularly as regards feeding and walking him, but despite this treatment he was fond of me. Seán used to bring his friends of the day round and three in particular used to come to the house and eat our food and drink our tea. Seán never knew they deliberately waited until he was out of the room before jeering at me, making jokes about me and laughing uproariously. Tiny could not stand this atmosphere and used to run around barking and trying to bite them. Finally he became so disturbed that I had to give him away to a local family. Perhaps it is my paranoia which accounts for my failure to understand how some people who have known me for many years still, for no reason I am aware of, treat me with suspicion and at times apparent dislike.

I had to begin looking after myself at the age of fifty-four. Prior to that I had always been looked after, going from home to hospital and to living with Nancy. I did not know what to do about everyday practical matters. I still slept in my clothes and did not wash or brush my teeth. I did not do any housework or gardening. I bought expensive delicacies and treats I could not afford or overbought mundane items. I took unnecessary taxis over the short distance between my house and the centre of March. I had no idea about money and was quite unable to pay bills; Niall had to deal with all my household affairs as I was not capable of having a cheque-book. In the end Ciarín told me it was time to take a grip on myself and shocked me out of my helplessness by making me aware of my true situation.

As I eventually began to recover my equilibrium and take some pride in my existence, I came to think that all that was required of me was to take my medication and, in recognition of the fact that I was devout as a child, to visit a Marian Centre roughly once a year and join in the communal activities when I was there as best I could. I did not find this custom too much for me and it seemed to impart an underlying continuity to my life.

I had finally taken up writing as a hobby in August 1987. My father had been suggesting it for years, though he never expected much to come of my writings, and others, friends and relatives, thought that to express myself in such a way would be good for me. Laurence had encouraged me by saying that it's never too late to do something like that, even for someone very severely schizophrenic. Until this point, as far as I was concerned, I was only fit for the grave, but from then on a new hope possessed me. My first piece was called 'Christ' and was supposed to be built around Christ's seven sentences spoken from the Cross. It turned out to be around 6,000 words from an evidently hyper-ill mind in the grip of extreme religious mania. Ciarín read it and called it 'unadulterated gibberish'. Then I began to write in earnest, with several attempts at my life-story and some fictional pieces. In December 1989 I was rewarded with a short publication, for which I had editorial help from Niall's wife, Monica: the Passage Day Centre for the Homeless in Kensington published the last paragraph of my 'Reflections on My Madness' in their Christmas newsletter. I was fortunate that Monica was a voluntary worker at the Passage and was able to use her influence with the nuns there. Dr Flood was pleased for me and I was elated with my taste of success. Until then the nearest I had come to using my literary skills had been in writing some personal letters; notably one of condolence in French to Michael's parents-in-law on the suicide of his manic-depressive sister-in-law, Martine, in 1977, which they much appreciated. When Éamonn Andrews died I wrote a letter of sympathy to Gráinne. My brother Niall told me that out of hundreds of such letters Gráinne felt mine to be one of the most consolatory. In 1990 I was delighted when my fifth attempt at my life-story impressed my family into insisting that I must keep on writing. That Christmas, Brian gave me a good idea for a story which I used when I returned home in the New Year. This was a humorous tale about two cousins, separated as children, who grew up in America and Ireland. As businessmen on the verge of ruin, they each spent a lot of time trying to impress the other with their success in the mistaken belief they would benefit financially. Neither ever realised the reality of the situation, though their wives saw through them immediately. I completed this story in May 1991 and called it 'Finucane's Folly'.

Between early autumn 1991 and August 1992, Dr Flood's successor, Professor Linford Rees, greatly improved my outlook on life by putting me on two courses of supplementary medication; a hormone treatment, called Sustanon, which I took for a short while. I had been becoming listless, which was, I believe, a result of my prolonged fight against the disease. Though Sustanon has side effects, it had the benefit of replacing my forty years of constant and intense suffering with an underlying feel-good factor and, at times, a sense of peace. By restoring some of the testosterone level I had lost as a result of taking my usual medication over many years, it renewed my general vitality and sense of well-being. Though most of the intended effects of this drug ceased a few years ago, some of the feel-good factor has remained. The severity of my illness ceased to matter to me as much as it had and this was aided by the fact that my illness was actually becoming a little milder.

In February 1992 I was very pleased indeed when a leading international magazine of the day called *For Him* published 'Finucane's Folly', for a fee of £150. I was lucky in having editorial help and constant encouragement with this piece and with many of my other literary efforts from Jim Dolamore and another great friend of my family, my brother Niall's first wife, Mary Falk.

I might have found the nine worst years of Nancy's and my married life less difficult to cope with, had I had a friend to confide in. Unlike Nancy, I had hardly any friends, apart from Joy, until 1992, some four years after Nancy's death. Various friends and members of my family began then to come many miles to stay the weekend, in nearly all cases for the first time. I had further good luck in 1992 when finally, following May's and Hilda's long-standing advice, I started to go for long daily walks to try and keep fit. Also my State pension increased by fifty per cent up to the correct amount.

I have sometimes asked myself if it was a coincidence that the two major and completely unexpected events in my life, which together undoubtedly saved my life, occurred in 1959 after my visit to Lourdes the previous year. If so, I wonder if my various unexpected strokes of good luck in 1992, albeit relatively minor, were also a coincidence, for in 1991 I had visited what is universally regarded as a unique Marian Centre at Medjugorje in Herzegovina, in the former Yugoslavia.

I tend to subscribe to Montaigne's view that whether our merits be great, or like my own, minor, we owe more love to God than to ourselves, and to the belief of Duns Scotus that when a man genuinely loves himself or any fellow-creature properly, he loves God the more. I remember with profound humility and gratitude that Nancy and I loved one another very much for seven years. Of recent years I have come to value myself as I did in my youth, having extended my powers of concentration as far as possible towards their undergraduate level and I believe that I have done the best I can.

My love for Seán has always been genuine and deeply felt; from the day he was born it has never diminished. One of my memories of him as a little boy comes from my Walsall teaching year. It was December 1967 and Seán was six. It had been snowing as I saw him off to school and he was wearing a pair of short woollen trousers knitted by Nancy. He said something reproving to me and without thinking I replied, 'Go on to school. You're only a little titch.' He burst into tears and, taken aback, I found myself trying hard to reassure him that I had not meant to hurt him and I still loved him very much. Eventually his tears subsided and he strode cheerfully off to school. I have long felt that Seán's inherited characteristics to an extent bypass Nancy and myself; he inherits my mother's gentleness and consideration for others, my paternal grandfather's gifts for mathematics and the sciences, my paternal grandmother's musical gifts and my father's artistic ones. His career involves maths and science and he finds great pleasure in playing the Spanish guitar and in art work as hobbies. In physical appearance he resembles my father's family. Seán has a good sense of humour and likes nothing better than to watch a good comedy programme on television with me, as he did with Nancy when she was alive. One trait he clearly inherits from Nancy is his willingness to be on the side of the underdog.

When Seán was a child Nancy used to say that the relationship between him and me would only come into its own when he was grown up. Thankfully, she lived long enough to see her words come true, though this relationship took a quantum leap forward again when Seán started to study for his degree at Plymouth University and accordingly became fully mature, both intellectually and emotionally. Nancy would have been proud to know that he has recently been awarded the BSc which she encouraged him to study for.

11. A measure of peace

In the early days of my illness I clung grimly to my memories, inaccurate though they probably were, of what I had been like before I fell ill, in a vain attempt to straighten out my thoughts. I convinced myself that I still could and would fulfil my own and other people's expectations. I was only waiting for the right moment, but even to my deluded mind the right moment never seemed to be in sight. My paranoid self-delusion appeared to offer the only chance I had of coping not only with my persistently low self-image but with life in general. I have realised recently that others, unlike myself, could see very clearly the hopelessness of my situation as early as 1957. This in itself is indicative of the fact that my handicap might easily be likened to someone being obliged always to wear a blindfold. I lived in a nightmare world which bore only a superficial resemblance to reality and thus reduced my ability to cope with simple routine situations even further. A key factor in schizophrenia is the patient's instability.

An offshoot of my low self-image was my equally irrational conviction that everyone, no matter who, had an irreversibly low opinion of me and nothing I could do would redeem me in their eyes. It was as if I was pinned to the ground by a boulder and all I could do was to bow myself under its crushing weight. My mind was acutely susceptible to pain; even after I began to use it again, the pain continued.

From the start of my illness in 1953 I felt guilty that my conscious self had been replaced by incompetence and blinding pain and it seemed that my predicament would have no end. I was full of agonising self-doubts and self-criticisms—pointlessly so, as I see today. Yet, paradoxically, I still clung to my paranoid and increasingly unrealistic image of myself as the intelligent and promising son of my distinguished parents.

Before I was given suitable medication in 1959 I tried hard not to demean this unrealistic self-image but failed for lack of the necessary psychological skills. I tried to guess at how I should behave in a given social situation. Everything was a major problem to me, from buying something in a shop to behaving with decorum at a formal dinner party. In the case of dinner parties, for example, I was for years afraid to eat more than a forkful or two of food lest my difference from others showed itself.

Even a few years later I was still capable of behaving very oddly. Before Niall's wedding to his first wife Mary in 1964, while I was in the car with Father Dónal and another great friend of my father's, the artist Pat Scott, travelling down to County Kerry from Dublin, I asked Father Dónal what would be expected of me as best man at the wedding. I expected a suggestion to the effect that, as a distinguished visitor from England, I should lend my weight to the proceedings by mingling freely with the other guests and by playing 'agony uncle' if any of them confided their problems to me. Though at the time I was deflated when he replied, 'Just behave with decorum', I wish now that I had been well enough to heed his advice.

After the wedding, I was overcome by symptoms of religious mania and anxiety during my speech and even urgently entreated Niall in front of the bemused guests to wait to make love to his new bride at least until they arrived at my father's Kenmare Bay cottage, their honeymoon destination an hour away. It is characteristic of my brother that he was understanding, and made light of the matter, getting me out of my predicament by saying I was merely trying to be amusing.

Strangers who treated me with the sympathy I needed were rare. I was glad when they responded to me with nothing more than indifference. The usual reaction to me was suspicion and hostility or belittlement. My instability gave rise to erratic movements, which showed I was different from others in a seemingly quite unacceptable way; my personality was so fragmented that it was impossible for me to prove that I was harmless despite my appearance.

Whenever people were frightened by my wild looks, I was always shocked and bewildered and felt guilty. I myself was fully aware I had no criminal intent but no one but my family and close friends seemed to understand. All I could do was to try to compensate for my physical presence by remaining as calm as possible. I always found that the effort was worth it, even if I was not to see the people concerned again.

For years it was very distressing for me if I was ever asked by a former fellow law-student at a social gathering in Dublin what I was currently doing. Common sense should have told me they all knew the history of my schizophrenia, with my initial illness, brief recovery and serious relapse. Instead, disorientated and blind to reality, I would conjure up the false image of the above-average student I had once been and persuade myself they saw me in the same light. I used to mutter that a marvellous job was in the pipeline, the nature of which I left unspecified. If, as happened sometimes, I was pressed further, my fragile defences would collapse and I would feel as though I were in the confessional as I admitted weakly that I was actually staying in a mental hospital at that moment. Deep feelings of inadequacy and hopelessness about my future would well up inside me as, albeit temporarily, my comfortable if self-delusory image of myself was once again shattered.

The barrister in question would usually react with a momentary flash of bitter disappointment in me; almost as if my lowly position reflected badly on him. He would soon mumble an excuse and hastily walk away. I would get the impression that I had ceased to exist in his eyes, or at least was of no consequence whatever. I imagined that later, when I was not there, if someone had asked him about me, it would have been with the utmost difficulty that he would have remembered I once had a place in his life. If this sort of conversation ever took place, I suspect it might have been closed by his adding, 'but no one knows what happened to him'.

Once I was in England and on medication, I used to try to act the part of how I thought a normal man would have behaved. For example, I tried to walk in the street without letting my footsteps or my body language appear disturbed. But owing to the severity of the complaint, my efforts tended to be unconvincing.

At the point in 1969 when there was no medication at all in my system, my presence tended either to alarm people or to cause them to belittle me to an even greater extent, because it was to be many years before any of the infrastructure of my psyche was rebuilt. To this day, without the medication I should not be able to concentrate at all; in fact I should be dependent on others to the point of not being able to perform the most basic of functions.

Unfortunately even today the best medication available still does not fully address the problem of restabilising the fragmented personality and powers of concentration of those severely ill with schizophrenia. The sufferer needs as much care and attention as a small child and the illness is extremely difficult to live with.

Is that me?

Most people in the early days of my illness seemed to be unaware that, even given the fact that my old self was even more repressed and unstable, I could certainly function on a level above
that of an animal, if only on a purely intellectual level. I could cope
with intellectual or academic work, for which normal practical adult
responsibilities had only a minimal relevance, providing I applied
myself rigorously to the matter in hand, but it took a few more
years before I became as mentally competent as I was to be when I
went to Leeds University. From 1965 onwards, my conscious mind
began to be able to express itself most clearly when I put something
in writing.

Even a kind-hearted person cannot see another's inner pain. Nor
can an X-ray detect it. I was always too withdrawn to be able to
assert my native self and indeed it had ceased to exist. I was an
empty and vulnerable shadow walking in the community. Until at
least 1992 many simple experiences were painful to me. The fact
that I liked to please people, as in my youth, but found I could
seldom do so, had the effect of compounding my over-anxiety and
sense of inadequacy.

In recent years the pain has come less from the illness than from
the reaction of others to my self-evident handicap. People look apprehensive and move away. In the last few years I have been able to
appreciate that, despite the seemingly remote and will-o'-the-wisp
existence of my old self, my achievement in getting my degree indicates that I do have a self or a soul. However, I did not find this
convincing before because my ability to know my own identity vis-
à-vis the identities of others had been fundamentally undermined; I
was unable to know myself or anyone else. Some time before Betty
died in 1963 I asked her what she thought about my long-term
future and she comforted me by saying that she felt sure that my

illness would considerably diminish, though she added, 'I think you'll always walk with a slight limp.' In the event, and happily, she was proved right: my limp, though some may think it pronounced, has caused me little or no distress in comparison with the blinding inner pain, which for years never left me.

Looking back at my worst years, I'm grateful that recently this inward pain has become a lot milder and my capacity to concentrate on running my life normally has been revived. In Bordeaux at Christmas 1991 Roger Hypoustèguy told me when he was giving me my injection, '*Il faut faire marcher la cervelle*', 'The brain needs exercise', meaning it is vitally important for true quality of life to extend one's mental muscles to their limit and beyond. I put the recent improvements in the quality of my life down to both my ongoing efforts to increase my concentration and to a relatively minor but definite renewal of the faith of my childhood.

For nearly thirty years not only had Nancy carried all domestic responsibilities physically, emotionally and psychologically, but I depended on her as a small child does on its mother. She pointed me in the right direction about everything, including carrying out simple matters like personal hygiene.

Between May 1988 and August 1992 I was like a ship without a tiller tossed about on a stormy sea. Thereafter I began to feel better; my writing was going well and I was proud of having been published. The new medication had left me with an increased feeling of well-being and I found for the first time that I could enjoy coping with normal daily activities when I needed to, which is mostly the case these days. The more routine the situation, social or personal, the more I enjoy dealing with it.

From 1992, as I became more at peace with myself, I came to see that, despite her most intense emotional sufferings, Nancy eventually realised that it was not my fault or hers or anyone's that, as it had transpired, I was never going to be well enough to fulfil our original dream. My relationship with Nancy was as vital as the medication in keeping me out of hospital for many years and this was still the case even when it had begun to deteriorate. I shall always be grateful to her for that.

Today I can understand that without our many years together I should have had no chance whatsoever of surviving, let alone of enjoying my present better quality of life. Had she known about my present improvement and that her two sons are doing well, I am sure Nancy would have felt that in her relatively short life she had achieved what for most partners in her situation would have been the impossible.

The year 1994 brought me even more peace of mind. My story-telling continued to give me great fulfilment and I felt I was writing better than I ever had. In March I was working on a story called 'Study in Grey', about two failed conmen who return a large sum of money to a titled lady, expecting a reward, and receive a copy of the Venerable Bede's *History of the Church of England* for their trouble. I found it hard to believe that I was capable of writing so well but it gave me a tremendous feeling of hope after all the despair. At the beginning of August I was sitting on my bed fiddling with the radio when suddenly a small inner voice, not at all like my psychotic hallucinations, spoke to me quietly and affectionately. I believe it was my mother's birthday and I would like to think it was she who said to me in a reassuring yet authoritative way, 'Leave it to me, Anthony. I know you can't do it without me.' The comfort of knowing she was watching over me was immense.

When Seán, Michael and I were touring Ireland in 1995 Michael pointed out that there is no underdog like a schizophrenic in today's world, especially when he's old. We visited Glenstal and met an old school friend of mine called Seán Johnson, who is now a Benedictine himself and an eminent scholar. I remembered him as a shy, studious boy with whom I had enjoyed many a stimulating discussion about books. Seán Johnson reminded me how popular I was at school; I had forgotten this over the many years of 'sticking out like a sore thumb' and it was comforting to hear this from someone who had known me before I fell ill. During our visit Father Columba told me he believed my son Seán and Michael were right to say I was one of those who had shared in Christ's Passion. I can say that Nancy did the same through her own suffering during the prolonged battle between her exceptional conscience and her tormented emotions.

Nancy may not have been my soul mate in the accepted sense, but she was the linchpin of my hold on life for nearly thirty years. Though my love for her may have been to a large extent a psychotic love, once it was enhanced by her unique response it sustained our happiness for many years.

She also gave me a normal son who provided me with an added incentive to keep going. If it had not been for Seán as the personification of everything we both most cherished, our relationship probably would not have lasted as long and my story would have remained untold. Seán is a constant reminder that, despite my unpromising handicap, Nancy saved me by being my partner when no one else I have ever known would have done so, through the good times and all the bad times.

For many years Nancy knew she would die before her time if she did not leave me. Life itself is the most precious blessing of all, and she gave up hers by looking after me when, for most of her last thirteen years after our return to March, and indeed for most of her nineteen years of neurosis and bronchial asthma, she was well enough to leave me and save herself. In that time she was often sorely tempted to do so but, knowing as she did that our son needed both his parents and that I could not possibly have survived without her, she listened to her conscience and stayed.

Few partners, knowing a thankless and potentially lethal situation for them could be avoided, would have sacrificed themselves for someone with my complaint in its ultra-severe form, especially had they been, for a long time, increasingly disillusioned and unhappy with a relationship that would inevitably, sooner or later, show itself as a source of discord. At the end she made her peace by gently saying some reassuring words to me about how she saw my life ahead, on my own. It was her way of giving me her last blessing, as before she had given me my first as a grown man.

In the last few years, for the first time in my adult life, my capacity to feel mental pain has been soothed and I have been at peace. Today I realise from long experience that my spirit did not cause my downfall and that fortunately it is itself, as others have told me, indestructible. My sister assures me, and all my family agree, that my 'gentle, true and real soul' remains unsullied by my illness in any of its manifestations. Perhaps the doctors in my life would feel they could say that their enlightened and inspired care has not been entirely wasted, when they compare the quality of my life of recent years with what it was when I first arrived in England in 1958.

Now

_____

My life today is a simple one, but I live life to the full, much as I did in my youth, albeit in a somewhat slower manner. I live in a small, detached bungalow by the River Nene. This river rises near Northampton and flows through Peterborough, March and Wisbech to its outlet in the Wash. An old bye-law describes the quiet street my house is in as a 'bridle path'. Formerly horse-drawn traffic could pass along it only when horses were led by the bridle. Today it is signposted 'Vehicle Access Only'.

The only room in my house with any claim to size is the living-room, which is south-facing; outside the French windows is a patio which leads down through a terraced garden to the boat jetty. On the opposite bank of the river is a park where ducks, geese, moorhens and swans, in season with their young, patrol the river. Occasionally, a kingfisher or heron is to be seen. Apart from children feeding the wildlife, the people most interested in the river are boatmen, navigating their narrow boats or cabin cruisers, and fishermen. Because their interests conflict, these two groups give me the impression of being in a constant state of armed neutrality. The view from my window is a constant source of pleasure.

I should say that I have a conspicuous vice, as unhealthy as it is unpopular, shared by an ever-shrinking minority of the population, namely, cigarette smoking. I mention my cigarettes here because they always have been and clearly will remain a part of my life-story, which I am here trying to tell 'warts and all'. I believe people with a psychiatric problem are prone to being smokers, perhaps because a cigarette can be a great comfort. I accept that I am addicted and try simply to indulge my habit without distressing those who have an aversion to it. Though I only smoke when I have nothing else to occupy me, I am philosophically resigned to the fact that I automatically mark out my days in cigarettes.

I suffer from religious mania as a consequence of my illness. My religious feelings come from the Christian faith rooted in my upbringing and only became a mania when I began to be psychotic in 1953. Unlike a fever or a spasm, this mania does not come and go, but constantly underlies my waking hours, being exacerbated in certain situations. It manifests itself through language and takes no other form as far as I am aware. Though I can generally keep it under control, I find my religious mania distressing and burdensome. This obsessive mental sickness was at its worst from the beginning of my illness until my second term at Leeds University in 1970. Then for a number of years until Nancy died it affected me a little less severely. I went to Mass intermittently, but, as in the previous years, my spirituality was born out of desperation and an anxiety to be normal. Since I began to visit the Marian Centre at Medjugorje regularly I have found going through the physical rituals of worship there comforting and healing, though on my return I tend to suffer from an extreme reaction. As I have explained, I feel that good things happen to me after Marian Centre visits and so my expectations are always too high. I become over-anxious and increasingly desperate when the longed-for miracle does not materialise and I torment myself with unanswerable questions about my continued existence and my place in the Almighty's plans.

Another symptom of mine which has not diminished in its

severity since I first became ill, is my obsessiveness over matters arising in my life which may not be important to anyone except me. This affects only myself and those close to me and, typically, might involve in one day five or six phone calls to the same person. I might, for instance, be constantly phoning a relative to issue an invitation to stay with me, ringing Seán or Brian to ask which of several words or phrases is the best way of expressing an idea or ringing anyone in the family to talk over anything under the sun. Not being fully my old self, even now I am unsure of myself. As a natural instinct of mine is to want to please others and as, with regard to my writings, I am also trying to please myself, I tend to become manically obsessed by almost any insignificant matter which may arise. However, even when some such matter is worrying me, it does not prevent me from going about my daily life, or from getting a good night's rest.

I tend to rise late these days, as I find I need a lot of sleep. After I have taken the inhalers I need for my relatively mild bronchial asthma and have eaten a small but adequate breakfast, the first thing I do is have a cigarette. I have lunch, again late, in a café east from my house in the town centre. After lunch, if I want to borrow a book, I return home via the lending library, where over the years I have found many rich pickings. The March Health Centre, where I am a regular visitor to the treatment room for my injections, to see my doctor or to collect a prescription, is a few yards to the west up my street. Further on again are my 'locals', where I go in the evenings to drink two or three pints of my favourite alcoholic brew and soak up the atmosphere. In the evening, too, I enjoy reading a wide range of literature and watching television. I also try to write creatively, for my own pleasure, or sometimes displeasure, when, being cruel to be kind, my 'quality control department' points out the error of my ways!

Is that me?

On Sundays I eat a traditional pub lunch. I get on well with the staff and other regular customers in all my usual haunts. I feel at home with the small circle of people whom I see regularly and I am extremely lucky to have caring and helpful neighbours who ensure that I am always in touch with someone who has my welfare at heart. As I am a creature of habit, I usually take two one-and-a-half mile walks a week. Not only do I enjoy this, I find I need it. As I write, I have been taking these constitutionals for over seven years. I find that the fact that I walk along the same streets each time is comfortable and reassuring. Many years ago I used to cycle and owned the sort of bicycle messenger boys rode then. Once, when I was rushing to take home some eggs in time for supper, I approached the traffic lights at the bridge at some speed, only to notice too late that the lights were already at amber. A distinguished local gentleman of nearly ninety, a neighbour of ours, was gingerly stepping on to the zebra crossing. Unable to stop, I shot past him with inches to spare and heard a muffled exclamation as he leapt back on to the kerb. He took extreme umbrage at this and told Nancy. At her request I sold my bicycle forthwith. Today I walk.

Since the early 1990s I have been fortunate in having a very good GP in Dr Thomas and a gifted psychiatrist in Dr Kilgour. I have an excellent relationship with both doctors. Dr Thomas told me recently that my psychosis had been so severe up to a few years ago that it could possibly have damaged my central nervous system. If this is so, it might explain at least some of my incompetence in practical matters. Unfortunately, Dr Thomas went on to say that I will always have to live with this, as there is nothing that can be done about it at this stage.

Exceptionally for a busy, highly-skilled psychiatrist, since Dr Kilgour lives nearby he visits my house to monitor my Modecate medication at regular intervals throughout the year. He makes every effort to improve my condition and recently he decided to give me the opportunity of trying a new drug of which he had high hopes. He took me off the Modecate at Christmas in 1997 and started me on Olanzapine, a drug which gives 75 per cent of sufferers a new life, free from most of the side-effects caused by fluorine, a constituent of the older drugs such as Modecate. These fortunate patients are released from the unreal world which they inhabit and become almost entirely their old selves again. Sadly, however, the Olanzapine did not work for me. I have been taking the fluorine-based drugs for too long, more than forty years, and now cannot manage without them, so in March 1998 I began having the Modecate injections again. Even so, I still like to think that, beyond my conscious mind, my subconscious psyche still offers a glimpse of wholesome, non-psychotic hope about my future, based on medication which would fully release my old self and stabilise it permanently.

Though Seán at present still lives in Plymouth, having taken his degree in Composite Engineering and Podiatry there, he visits me two or three times a year and for the rest he and I are in constant touch by phone and letter. My feelings for him vis-à-vis my other relationships are unique because he derives partly from myself. I alone am able to give him the moral support he needs if something important goes wrong, in much the same way as my mother, Nancy and Ciarín have done for me, and it is a truly wonderful feeling for me to know that, at least until he got his degree, he needed me virtually to the point of remaining alive. Fortunately, now he is successful and fulfilled. He has patented and is currently working on his own design for a boot to prevent diabetics getting severe foot ulcers. My obsessiveness about various matters is virtually non-existent in my dealings with Seán.

The company of my friends and relatives is important to me and

I enjoy visiting them and having them visit me. I make regular trips to see my brothers and sister and go away on holiday several times a year, either in Britain or Ireland or further afield. As I write I have just returned from an invigorating walking holiday, six-and-a-half thousand feet up in the Austrian Tyrol.

After Seán, the closest person to me is Ciarín. When my mother died in 1976, Ciarín equally successfully took over her role in my life and supports me all she can. I am extremely dependent on her. Her efforts to help me have constantly surpassed everything in my life my mother could possibly have wished for me. When I was sixty in November 1993, friends and relatives came from all round England and several from Ireland, Spain and the Channel Islands at her invitation, for a very special dinner party to launch me into the sexagenarian set. But, to show that even Ciarín is human, I must say that she occasionally loses her temper with me when I become hopelessly obsessive about some insignificant matter. At such times she shouts long and hard at me, often on the phone, until my reason finally takes over again. Ciarín keeps a keen eye on my quality of life and in particular on my health.

The passage of time and geographical separation have not dimmed my feelings for my brother Michael, the closest brother to me in age, with whom I shared all my childhood experiences. We have never exchanged an angry word. I have always had a good relationship with my brothers Brian and Niall, though they both came into my life in an even more significant way after I lost Nancy and I enjoy their company enormously. Brian and his wife Nesta stayed with me a couple of years ago shortly after they were married and Niall drives up to see me from his office in London at least once a year. Both brothers phone me regularly to find out how I am faring. Brian is incredibly kind and gentle like my mother and is always available at the end of the phone to listen to my problems. I know that I can call on him at any time for help and advice and, like Seán's, his patience has been infinite over helping me with the choice of individual words and phrases for this book. Niall helps me with the practical and financial aspects of my life; his help with the building of my house was invaluable and he continues to work hard on my behalf in a variety of ways. He deserves all the success he has enjoyed in his own life.

I am told that my brothers find it extremely painful to reconcile their memory of the vital and charismatic figure whom they admired with the broken and confused character I became at the age of twenty. I am lucky that Ciarín, whose childhood memories of me begin only with the early stages of my illness, has a less emotional response to my situation and is thus more easily able to co-ordinate the family's concern for my welfare. My life would be of a considerably lower quality without my siblings being on my side and I thank them for all their love and care.

All my sisters-in-law are wonderfully supportive and I appreciate everything they do for me. Colette and her family have always looked after me well when I have visited them in France and made me feel that their home is mine. Nesta and Monica invite me over to Ireland two or three times a year each and are extremely hospitable and kind hosts. Nesta is gentle and caring, like Brian, and I am happy that he has found such a lovely wife. Monica is generous to a fault and always on my side; when I stay with her and Niall she makes a tremendous effort to make everything a special treat. I am still in touch with my ex-sister-in-law, Mary, who was of enormous help to me in revising my earlier writings and who is the only person outside my immediate family to provide consistent financial help when it was needed.

Is that me?

Many people have given me help with my writing over the years and I am grateful to all of them. My cousins, the Brittains – my Aunt Betty's children – have always given me their time and shown great interest in my projects. Peter has constantly encouraged me to write, Patrick and his wife Margaret read many early drafts of my stories and have often shown me marvellous hospitality. Judy and Betty have been equally generous with their help and advice on many occasions and Betty has been especially kind with her comments on this book.

I owe thanks to my niece, Cara, who in the last few years has given me much encouragement and who has been happy to apply her literary acumen to these pages, thus showing me what potential she has as a writer. I am particularly grateful to Ciarín, who has given me guidance at every stage and a great deal of trenchant general advice. Without Ciarín's help and hard work I doubt if I should have come even close to finishing my story.

In this narrative I have done no more than relate my life experience. It has been easier to recount the events which have made up my life than to analyse the painful and disorientating symptoms of my illness; during my worst breakdowns my mind was filled with emptiness and the fragmenting of my conscious self makes description difficult. If my story sheds any light on paranoid schizophrenic illness from a patient's viewpoint and thereby helps my fellow sufferers, I shall feel my life has been the more worthwhile.

I think I shall enjoy a couple of pints of Guinness this evening; maybe in the morning I shall at last recognise the man in the shaving mirror as an old friend.

July 1999

Postscript

Ciarín Scott

My brother died unexpectedly on 3 February 2000. He had finished 'Anthony's Story' the previous summer and it was returned to him that October edited and ready for his comments. He was grateful for Susan Dolamore's excellent work and in particular her sensitivity in allowing him to retain his own voice throughout.

Family and friends who read the typescript at this time responded with congratulations and praise and the accolades he received delighted him. Anthony knew that in writing his story, with all the painstaking effort this had required, he had been able to overcome the challenges of his hard life. His sense of achievement against all the odds gave his voice lightness in the last months and he laughed a lot.

Anthony was also really content in his daily life. He had kind and attentive neighbours and had found a warm and genuinely welcoming pub in The Ship, where he was much sought after at quiz time for his general knowledge. In November 1999 he went to Medjugorje with Seán and their visit was a great success. Anthony returned radiating spiritual peace and a new restfulness. In December he went to Seán's graduation, which he said made him happy and proud beyond words. He and Seán spent Christmas and New Year together at home in March for the first time in years. He had always wanted to go to Antarctica and was in the middle of planning a cruise there. Considering his illness and his dependence on medication, he showed bravery and an adventurous spirit in working out the arrangements.

Two days before he died Anthony told us all how he had dreamt about Nancy the night before. In the dream they were having a picnic as they had had in the old days. This dream seemed to embody the essence of the love they shared in their first seven years together and banished the memories of their difficult latter years. He had woken with a glow of happiness, which stayed with him and followed him throughout that day. Next day he was still talking about it at lunch in the pub. That night he died in his sleep; it seemed to us as if Nancy had been calling him. He had prayed in Medjugorje for a peaceful death and his prayers had been answered.

There was a requiem Mass for him in the church in March where Nancy was buried, which was attended by all the family, and his friends and neighbours. Seán picked snowdrops for the coffin and arranged the flowers in the church. He spoke movingly about how he would miss his father and what it had meant seeing his broken mind coming together in the last years. We held a splendid wake for Anthony at The Ship and many pints of Guinness were drunk to him; he would have loved it. As he had wanted, we then took him home for the funeral to Ireland, where friends, including those from his university days, paid their respects. He was buried beside our mother, grandparents and Aunt Betty.

In all the letters and comments we have had since Anthony's death, there are recurring themes: his caring sweetness; his inability to say an unkind word about anyone; his courtesy, gentleness and quality of innocence; his courage and lack of self-pity. It was remembered that, despite the length and intensity of his pain, he never lost his delightful wit and sense of humour. When Anthony laughed, his face would light up with unexpected joy. Over the ten days we were together after his death we all felt we could hear his wonderful distinctive laugh.

He never complained about his illness and had with dignity made the very best of his life. His ambition to write his own story had given him hope in the dark days after Nancy's death and when the faint possibility of realising his dream turned into a solid achievement, it transformed his existence. He always believed that he was going to get better and that deep inside he still had the same vibrant personality as in the years before his illness; it was his resolution to show the world how much he had struggled to keep this personality alive that enabled him to keep going.

Anthony was immensely relieved to have completed his self-imposed task and was excited about what he had accomplished and looking forward to his story being published. He died a few days after making his final amendments.

November 2000